# The
# Jigsaw/Scroll Saw Book
## with 80 Patterns

## R. J. De Cristoforo

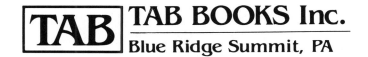

TAB BOOKS Inc.
Blue Ridge Summit, PA

FIRST EDITION
FIRST PRINTING

Copyright © 1990 by **TAB BOOKS Inc.**
Printed in the United States of America

Reproduction or publication of the content in any manner, without express
permission of the publisher, is prohibited. The publisher takes no responsibility for
the use of any of the materials or methods described in this book, or for the
products thereof. Printed in the United States of America.

**Library of Congress Cataloging-in-Publication Data**

DeCristoforo, R.J.
    The jigsaw/scroll book, with 80 patterns / by R.J. DeCristoforo.
        p.   cm.
    ISBN 0-8306-9269-X      ISBN 0-8306-3269-7 (pbk.)
    1. Jig saws.   2. Woodwork   I. Title.
TT186.H428   1989
684′.083—dc20                                                89-20205
                                                                    CIP

TAB BOOKS Inc. offers software for sale. For information and a catalog, please
contact TAB Software Department, Blue Ridge Summit, PA 17294-0850.

Questions regarding the content of this book should be addressed to:

    **Reader Inquiry Branch
    TAB BOOKS Inc.
    Blue Ridge Summit, PA 17294-0214**

Kimberly Tabor: Acquisitions Editor
Eileen P. Baylus: Technical Editor
Katherine Brown: Production
Lori E. Schlosser: Cover Design

Cover photograph courtesy of Delta International Machinery Corporation.

# Contents

# Introduction

IF THERE IS ONE POWER TOOL WITH WHICH BOTH SHOP INSTRUCTORS AND PROFESSIONAL woodworkers do not hesitate to suggest as a starting machine for aspiring woodworkers, young and old, it would be the scroll saw—or is it jigsaw? Veteran power tool users think "jigsaw," and dictionaries list both "scroll saw" and "jigsaw," the distinction one gathers being that "scroll saw" applies to the blade, which is "narrow" or "ribbon like" and is held in a frame and moved up-and-down to cut curves and ornamental designs. The description continues with "such a saw mounted in a power-driven machine." Then to the jigsaw entry; "an electric machine with a narrow blade," and so on . . .

Even among manufacturers who have generally adopted the term *scroll saw*, you can find deviations, such as listing some blades for the machine as *jigsaw blades*. Although in some literature you might discover an attempt to go for scroll saw puzzles, it will take a couple of generations to get away from jigsaw puzzles.

Everyone seems to agree that *scroll work* and *scroll*, as they apply to sawing, have to do with ornamental work that features scrolls and spirals as the basic design, a definition that might be so, but that does not begin to tell what the machine can do. Anyway, for the book, I go along with the current trend; we'll talk about the scroll saw.

The major illusion regarding the machine has to do with its exclusiveness in the areas of intricate sawing and *piercing*, the latter being the function that allows internal design openings without an entry cut from an edge of the stock. The fact that it can handle blades that are so fine they practically can turn on themselves—an application that is necessary for the intricacies of inlaying and marquetry—has led to the tool's image of an "arty" machine, used strictly for gentle crafts and hobbies.

The scroll saw's contribution in these areas is impressive. However, because the average, modern machine can work with blades as wide as 1/4 inch, as well as those that are practically hairlike in cross section, and because depth of cut in hard and soft wood, and some other materials, is ordinarily 2 inches or more, it becomes obvious that the scroll saw is a practical tool for general accessory woodworking operations. You can use it to produce curved furniture components, even small-size cabriole legs—jobs you can't do on other tools like table and radial arm saws.

An enviable facet of the scroll saw is that it can be a one-tool shop. You don't need much else in the way of power equipment to complete projects that can range from purely decorative to highly practical—items that contribute to the home, are ideal for gift-giving, or are especially suitable as the output of a small cottage industry.

Toys, photo silhouettes, models, bird houses and feeders, lawn ornaments, and custom-designed signs and house numbers are among the popular projects that are fun to make and that can produce spare- or full-time income.

The average worker soon becomes enthralled with scroll sawing. He acquires skill and discovers techniques that lead to producing provocative pieces that can be considered works of art.

The scroll saw requires little room and no special environment. Compared with many other power tools, it makes little noise, and sawdust is easily controlled. Most products are compact and light enough so that, even when securely mounted on an independent stand, they are easily stored. The scroll saw is an intriguing tool and a nice machine for introducing a youngster to woodworking—under supervision, of course!

Much is said about the scroll saw being a "safe" machine. This is a bad choice of words because the tool works with power and toothed blades that can cut hard materials, so it can cut you. It's true that an accident with a scroll saw can cause less damage than is possible on other sawing tools, but the point is that no accident, no matter how slight, should occur.

Safety is, or should be, as much in the mind of the operator as it is in the tool and its guards. Feeling "safe" can lead to trouble. Always be alert, aware that any machine is disinterested in what you place in the path of the cutting component.

# Chapter 1

# The Tool

**T**HE MODERN SCROLL SAW IS QUITE A DEPARTURE FROM THE EXAMPLES THAT BECAME available after the concept was conceived. It is historically correct that many first saw mills produced boards of particular width by using straight, parallel saw blades that were secured in a frame and that moved up and down to perform—a reciprocating action that is pretty much the way today's scroll saws operate.

Most of the original products, while ingenious, were, by today's standards, rather crudely made affairs that consisted mostly of custom-designed wooden parts. Tension for a crude saw blade was supplied by a springy length of wood, or some similar elementary device, that was attached to an overhead structure of the machine of even to the ceiling of the workshop.

The operator was able to cause a downward movement of the blade by pumping a treadle. Getting the blade to return to the top of the "stroke" so the operator could pull it down again was the function of the flexible wooden arm. Because sawing occurred only when the blade moved downward, the blade was installed so its teeth pointed toward the table—which is exactly the situation that exists today.

Power, in early machines, was supplied by the operator, working a treadle or paddle-type affair or pumping a wheel as if he were riding a bicycle. A popular machine that appeared much later (circa 1923), maybe the prototype of what is now available, was powered by a hand crank and sold for about $6. Imagine applying power for the tool with one hand while the other hand guided the work! Later, the same machine was available with an integral motor and that made the price go up to about $20. The nation was experiencing a rough depression, but nevertheless, supply did not always keep up with the demand.

1

It is said that the tool, together with the existing depression, is what led to the jigsaw puzzle craze of that period. Many people, with minimum expenditure and expertise, were able to start a money-making business supplying puzzles. Today, by choice or necessity, it is not unusual to discover people following the same example—making money, part- or full-time, with a scroll saw as the major piece of shop equipment.

It is generally believed that what we accept today as good scroll saw blades came about through the vision and talent of a German craftsman (c. 1500). The slim blades were meant to be used in small frames for sawing by hand. Not much has changed in that area because hand operated *coping saws* are as popular as ever.

Actually, a look at a coping saw tells much about the way a scroll saw functions. The blade, in this case with pin-type ends, is secured in a U-shaped frame (Fig. 1-1). You can control tautness of the blade by turning the handle of the tool. The blade is adjustable for various cut directions and, because it can be mounted in its frame *after* it has passed through an entry hole in the stock, can be used for ''piercing'' (Fig. 1-2).

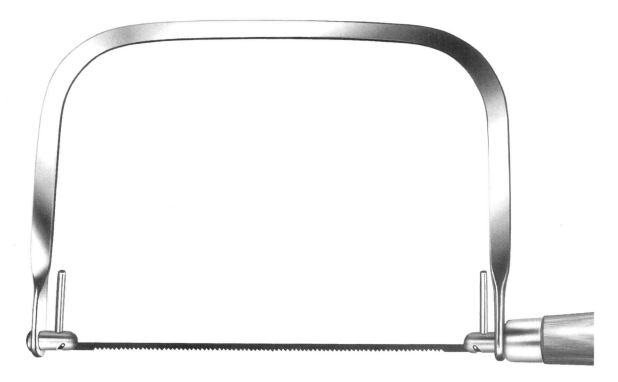

*Fig. 1-1.* First efficient scroll saw blades were made for hand-sawing in frames similar to this. *Coping saws*, as they are called, are still popular.

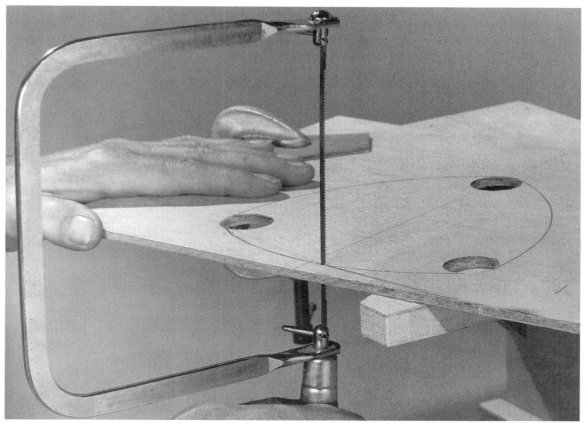

*Fig. 1-2. Piercing* is possible because the blade can be passed through predrilled holes in the stock before it is mounted in the frame. This factor applies to motorized scroll saws.

Similar frames for fine saw blades are called *jewelers saws* and *fret saws*. Jewelers saws work with plain-end blades and are highly recommended for use with metal piercing blades for the intricate detailing that is required when creating jewelry. Fret saws, because most of them have deep, U-shaped frames, are popular for hand scroll work where cutting is required far from an edge of the workpiece. Whatever is feasible with any of the hand frames is possible with powered scroll saws, but with greater convenience, easier-to-achieve accuracy, and, certainly, much less effort.

## MECHANICS OF THE SCROLL SAW

The engineering of a scroll saw must provide for converting the rotary action of an electric motor to the vertical, reciprocal movement that is needed for the blade to function. One method that accomplishes this, but that is not applicable to all machines, is shown in elementary fashion in Fig. 1-3. The cam, with its eccentrically mounted shaft, causes the housing and its attached spindle to move up and down.

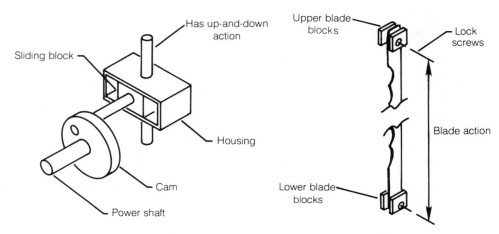

*Fig. 1-3.* The design of a scroll saw must provide for converting a motor's rotary action into the up-and-down movement needed by the saw blade. Designs of this type apply to saws with fixed arms.

When a blade is secured to the spindle with some sort of clamping device, it duplicates the action.

### Fixed-Arm Saws

Most tools that employ this type of mechanism have fixed upper arms; the only visible action is the blade's vertical movements. Because power, in essence, is delivered to the blade on the down stroke, a means of returning the blade to up position is provided. This is a plunger assembly, commonly, a tubular-encased, heavy-duty spring similar to what is shown in Fig. 1-4. The spring is compressed on the down stroke and then expands to original shape to return the blade.

The plunger actually does double duty. The higher it is positioned in its housing, the more tension is applied to the blade—the more the blade is "stretched" between upper and lower blade clamps (Fig. 1-5). On some products, such as the Delta fixed arm unit, the tubular case has graduations that can be used to establish tension in relation to the blade that is mounted and the material plus its thickness that is being sawed (Fig. 1-6). Usually, whatever the design of the tool, most efficient blade tension is in the operator's judgment. Optimum tension leads to easier, more accurate cutting, and longer blade life. This is part and parcel of scroll saw operating. Anyone using a scroll saw for a period of time acquires knowledge about the "just right" tension required for the blade and the operation.

A feature of many fixed-arm machines is that the upper arm can be swung aside or removed so that *saber sawing*, an application accomplished with stiff blades that are secured in only the lower chuck, can be done on oversize workpieces. Examples of fixed-arm machines that can be used in this fashion are shown in Figs. 1-7 through 1-9. I will talk more about the process of saber sawing in chapter 9.

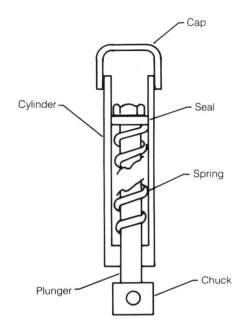

Cap

Cylinder

Seal

Spring

Plunger

Chuck

*Fig. 1-4.* A spring-loaded plunger assembly is used to return the blade on fixed-arm machines that power the blade only on the down stroke.

## Constant-tension Saws

Another area of scroll saw mechanisms, one that has caught the fancy of manufacturers and users alike, employs a rocker-type action that does much to ensure uniform blade tension. Thus, designs of this nature are often called *constant-tension* saws. The blades do not rely on a spring return. Instead, they are locked between arms that have a fixed relationship so the blade is powered on both up and down strokes.

In this area, there are two basic versions. One has a one-piece C- or U-shaped frame with a tensioning adjustment at the blade end of the arms; the other has separate parallel arms that pivot in unison and with the tensioning adjustment situated at the rear of the structure. It is convenient to be able to "stretch" the blade without reaching to the back of the machine, but whether this is a crucial factor in choosing a tool is a moot point. There are many other factors to consider.

The parallel-arm mechanism is highly respected by professionals and amateur woodworkers. Figure 1-10 shows the action of "twin" arms synchronized in a way that allows the blade to move vertically throughout the stroke. There is a slight forward travel when the blade moves down, and it is reversed on the up stroke. This minimizes friction, a contribution to longer blade life, and helps to dispose of sawdust very quickly.

The C-arm design (Fig. 1-11) has a different blade action. Because of the manner in which the arm pivots, the blade will angle slightly backward on its up stroke. In some cases, depending on the location of the arm's pivot point, the blade will slant

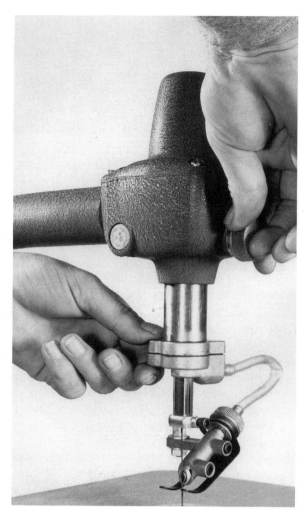

Fig. 1-5. The plunger assembly can be locked at various heights to provide adequate tension for the saw blade and the work being done.

Fig. 1-6. On some machines, such as the Delta fixed-arm tool, graduations serve as tensioning guides. The operator can prejudge acceptable tension when he is repeating an operation.

slightly forward of vertical when the down stroke is complete. This might be bothersome, but not critical, when sawing thick stock and the pattern involves abrupt, irregular curve sawing. It is not a negative factor on thin materials, or when following straight lines and gentle curves in thick stock.

## BLADE MOUNTING

On both C-arm and parallel-arm machines, the blade can't be clamped in a fixed position as it is on fixed-arm tools. If the blade was clamped it would bend at clamp-

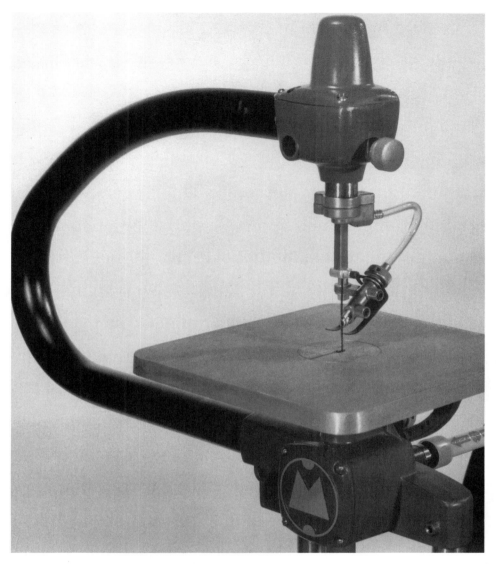

***Fig. 1-7.*** The original Shopsmith jigsaw has a tubular C-arm that can be removed or pivoted 90 degrees. Here, the tool is shown being powered by the Shopsmith multipurpose machine.

ing points on each stroke and this would, for one thing, result in premature blade breakage. The solution is to provide a means of allowing top and bottom blade clamps to pivot freely. The clamps can be V-shaped to sit in matching forms in the arms, or they can be mounted on pivot rods that provide the same necessary action. Some of the systems that are prevalent today are shown in Fig. 1-12.

Although constant-tension saws are getting significant attention these days, the fixed-arm design has not disappeared. A Delta, 24-inch, fixed-arm unit has been an

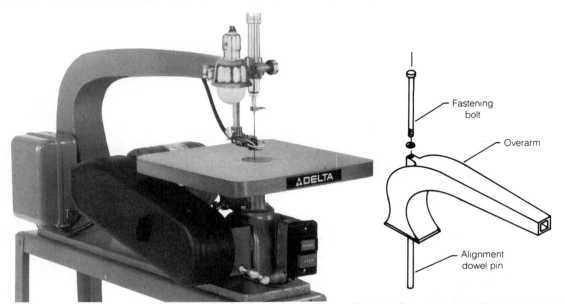

**Fig. 1-8.** The Delta fixed-arm unit has a removable upper arm so saber sawing on extra large workpieces can be performed.

**Fig. 1-9.** The arm on the Delta tool is removed by loosening one long bolt. A dowel pin serves to align the arm when it is replaced.

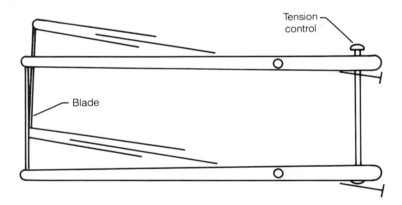

**Fig. 1-10.** On parallel-arm designs, "twin" arms move in unison in an action that provides vertical blade movement throughout the stroke.

ally in my shop for better than thirty years and, although I have added more "modern" concepts, I'm not about to discard the old friend. In fact, I know several skilled professionals and a few hobbyists, some of whom have become acquainted with the techniques of scroll sawing on fixed-arm machines, who are also adamant about not discarding the tool. One friend is a marquetry and inlay artist and he will defend the fixed-arm tool against all comers. He does ask that the machine have efficient speeds, preferably variable, and that the design include good blade chucks and efficient guides.

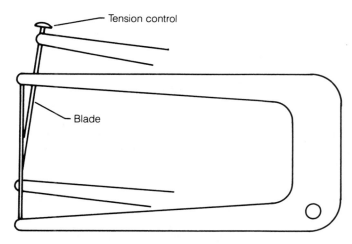

*Fig. 1-11.* On a C-arm design, the blade will angle backward a bit on its "up" stroke. Much of the blade's movement will depend on the location of the arm's pivot point.

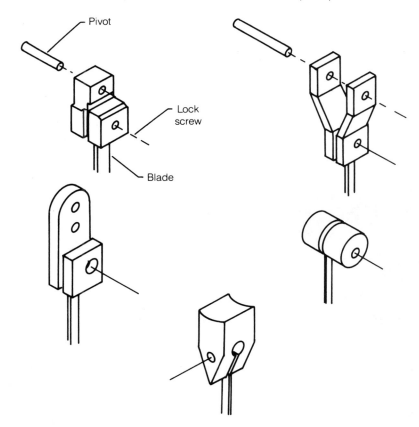

*Fig. 1-12.* Some of the blade-mounting systems that are found on constant-tension saws. Each is designed to allow the blade clamps to pivot.

The interest in fixed-arm versions seems to have influenced manufacturers as well as users because "old" fixed-arm machines are available, some with added features, and new ones are being offered.

## SIZES

The size of a scroll saw is designated by its throat capacity, which is the free distance from the rear structure to the blade (Fig. 1-13). The dimension is one half the width of work you can handle. For example, on a 15-inch machine you can cut to the center of a panel that is 30 inches wide. This is fact in terms of saw size but not realistic in terms of scroll sawing. Once you get to the center of the panel and need to make a turn to the left or right, the arm would interfere with rotating the workpiece. As far as straight cuts are concerned, however, some machines allow situating the blade 90 degrees from its normal position so work can be moved parallel to the front edge of the table. There also are special techniques that permit this, so, in the example we've presented, you would be able to "rip" down the center of a 30-inch-wide panel regardless of its length.

## TABLES

Manufacturers don't seem to agree on the ideal size and shape of scroll-saw tables. The depth of a table can't be more than what the throat capacity allows and some units go almost the whole distance, although others stop far short of it. Shapes include squares and rectangles, forms such as oversize ping pong paddles, even

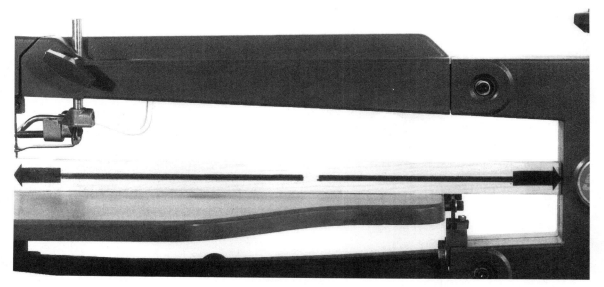

*Fig. 1-13.* The size of the scroll saw is designated by the open distance between the blade and the rear structure—in this case, on the new Shopsmith product, a generous 20 inches.

circular forms such as the one on the new Delta machine (Fig. 1-14). Delta says, "Round table shape allows the use of the table edge as a reference guide when rotating workpieces around the blade," which might be so, but more important is the mechanics of the table that allow, in addition to normal tilts left and right, an up and down tilt after the table has been rotated 90 degrees. This additional flexibility comes in handy on some complicated cutting procedures such as those, for example, required to produce dovetail joints.

A larger than average table does provide more work support, but it's possible you might never do scroll sawing on oversize workpieces and, when necessary you can always provide some outboard support. Anyway, once you decide on the tool you want, you take the table that goes along with it. Do check for an acceptable tilt range; preferably through 45 degrees one way and 15 degrees or more in the opposite direction.

## BLADE STROKE

Stroke is the vertical travel of the blade. This can range, on different machines, from about $3/8$ inch to better than 1 inch. If there is an average, it would fall somewhere between $3/4$ inch and 1 inch. It's obvious that a long stroke allows more saw teeth to work and this is an advantage generally, and especially when sawing thick stock with a heavy blade. A short stroke is more efficient when sawing thin materials, such as veneers. Most saws provide for a specific stroke, but there are exceptions. Some Hegner tools include adjustments so stroke length can be changed. An improvisation that is utilized by many workers that, in effect, shortens a blade stroke, is to attach an auxiliary platform to the tool's table. This does not really reduce stroke length, but it does provide for fewer saw teeth to contact the work.

## SPEEDS

The speed of a scroll saw is designated as the blade's cutting strokes per minute (CS/M, or sometimes simply SPM). Many saws have a direct drive system so the CS/M match the revolutions per minute (RPM) of the motor. Saws that provide for various speeds, which is advantageous in many areas of scroll sawing, do so with a mechanical device that provides a set of specific speeds, or even variable speeds, or, as is happening of late, by incorporating electronic, solid state controllers that provide variable speeds by turning a dial (Fig. 1-15). Sensors in the unit recognize and adjust speed and torque to maintain an efficient level of cutting performance, and this occurs even as cutting conditions change. A digital display reveals the CS/M.

A mechanical speed-changing device can be a set of cone pulleys connected with a V-belt, which would be capable of a number of specific speeds, or a movable sheave (variable drive pulley) that, in effect, provides infinitely variable pulley sizes so that by turning a crank any speed between minimum and maximum is available.

*Fig. 1-14.* The new Delta scroll saw has a circular table that can be rotated 90 degrees and tilted left and right and forward and back.

*Fig. 1-15.* Electronic controllers are found on many machines or they might be available as accessories. They provide an easy method of choosing the optimum speed for particular applications.

## EXAMPLES OF AVAILABLE SCROLL SAWS

Delta's fixed-arm scroll saw (Fig. 1-16) is a rugged machine that is found in school and professional shops, and that is popular with many amateurs. This is the unit, or its forebear, that has served happily in my shop for many years. Its 24-inch throat capacity plus its removable upper arm, allow scroll sawing, or saber sawing, on just about any size workpiece. Depth-of-cut capacity is $1^3/_4$ inches and it can easily handle blades as wide as $1/_4$ inch. Of course, as any scroll saw must, it allows passing blades through predrilled holes in the stock so piercing can be performed (Fig. 1-17).

The tool's lower chuck is unique (Fig. 1-18) because it will accommodate more than just conventional saw blades, machine files, sanding sticks, heavy saber saws, and the like. Also, it can be rotated 90 degrees so that, in unison with the upper chuck, blades will be parallel with the front edge of the table so you can make cuts of unlimited length. When organized for saber sawing, which can be accomplished with or without the upper arm, the blade is supported under the table. If the upper arm is not removed, the blade can be supported top and bottom (Fig. 1-19).

*Fig. 1-16.* Delta's fixed-arm product has been around for many years. Some features have been added to current offerings, but the basic structure is the same.

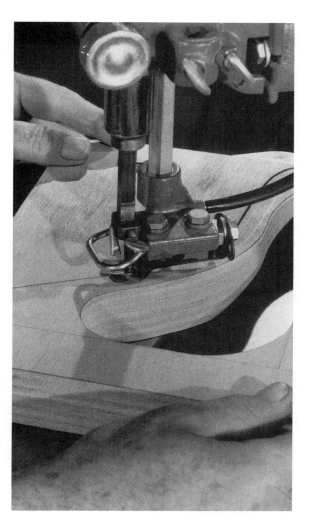

*Fig. 1-17.* The Delta fixed-arm tool sawing through a "pad" of 6 pieces of ¼-inch plywood. Sawed edges are pretty acceptable even though a wide blade is being used.

Good accessories include a special chuck that will automatically center fine blades, and individual blade guides that match the thickness of the blade in use (Fig. 1-20). These extras are especially useful when sawing puzzles and doing other chores, such as inlaying and marquetry.

The machine has a 1-inch stroke and is available with four specific speeds of 610, 910, 1255, and 1725 CS/M, or with a mechanical variable speed mechanism with a range of 650 to 1700 CS/M. The table is 14 inches square and can be tilted 45 degrees right, 15 degrees left, and 45 degrees front. The front-tilt feature allows bevel cutting on extra-long stock.

The upper mechanism includes an adjustable air blower, blade backup, a turret guide with slots for various blade thicknesses, and a spring hold-down that can be set to function even on bevel cuts (Fig. 1-21).

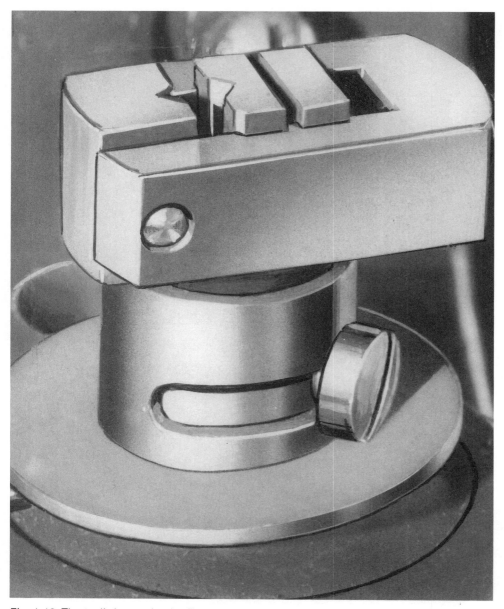

*Fig. 1-18.* The tool's lower chuck will accept round-shank tools like machine files and sanding sticks in addition to saw blades. The chuck also can be rotated 90 degrees.

Delta has taken a giant step into the area of modern scroll-saw design by introducing the 18-inch, C-arm machine that is shown in Figs. 1-22 and 1-23. The tool has several unique and practical features. One of the more impressive is the electronic solid state control station that is shown in Fig. 1-24. The component provides

*Fig. 1-19.* When saber sawing without removing the upper arm, the blade is supported both under and over the table.

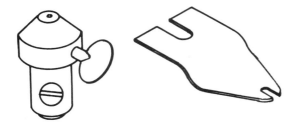

*Fig. 1-20.* A replacement for the lower chuck is a device that will automatically center fine blades. Individual guides that suite the width and thickness of various blades also are available.

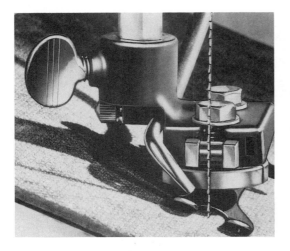

*Fig. 1-21.* The upper mechanism consists of a turret blade-guide, roller backup, air blower, and a spring-type hold-down that can be adjusted for bevel cutting.

*Fig. 1-22.* Delta's 18-inch entry into the constant tension saw arena. The tool is supplied with an electronic speed control with a range of 40 to 2000 CS/M.

infinitely variable speeds of 40 to 2000 CS/M, and incorporates a digital display that reveals the speed of the blade. This is helpful because the operator can chart the optimum speed for various blades and materials that he has learned from experience. What it means, for one thing, is that the saw can be preset to an efficient speed whenever an operation is being duplicated.

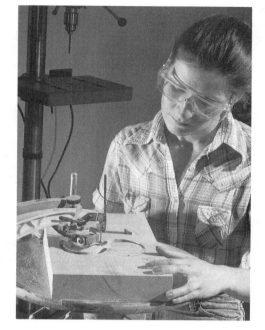

*Fig. 1-23.* The unit has a 2-inch depth of cut and works with standard 5-inch, plain-end blades. Blade stroke equals $^7/_8$ inch.

*Fig. 1-24.* The digital display that is part of the electronic control allows presetting to the optimum speed for a particular job (learned from experience) before work starts.

A second feature is the tool's 16-inch-diameter table that is as flexible as such a unit can be (Fig. 1-25). It can be tilted 45 degrees right, 30 degrees left, 15 degrees down at the back, and 30 degrees down at the front. This kind of freedom can facilitate many scroll-saw operations.

Blade tension is controlled by a knob at the front of the machine. In addition, there is a lever that is used to release the preset tension but without disturbing it (Fig. 1-26). Thus, when you wish to change from a dull blade to a similar sharp one, or need to replace a broken blade, you can do so and easily return to the tension you originally established. The device is especially handy when a project requires a number of piercing cuts. Usually, the blade requires retensioning each time it is released so it can be passed through an entry hole. With the lever, the correct, initial tension is quickly supplied. The series of steps shown in Figs. 1-27 through Fig. 1-29 demonstrates the procedure.

*Fig. 1-25.* The circular table is as flexible as such a unit can be. Tilt it left, right, forward, back; even rotate it—complete freedom that is helpful on many applications.

Accessories for the tool include a steel stand, lamp attachment, special blade holders so the blade can be used 90 degrees from its normal position, and a variety of blades for wood and metal sawing.

Apparently, Delta, by offering the 15-inch unit that is shown in Fig. 1-30, has not overlooked the group of woodworkers who seek a respectable machine without having to strain to pay for it. I saw this unit recently in a craftsman's catalog for about $140. The fact that it costs much less than other exotic versions that have additional functional features does not mean that it can't be used for efficient scroll sawing. In fact, the design is based on parallel arms, which means constant tension, and tensioning methods and blade mounting systems are similar to those employed on higher priced machines.

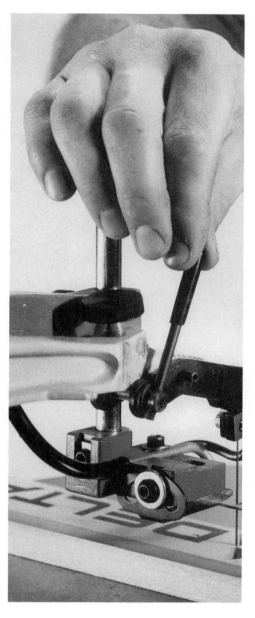

*Fig. 1-26.* A lever, at the front of the upper arm, is used to release an established blade tension. Thus, when doing piercing or replacing a blade, you can automatically return to the tension that is right for the job.

The tool functions with a direct drive 1.6 amp motor that delivers 1725 CS/M and it permits a 2-inch depth of cut. The 17-inch × about 8-inch cast iron table tilts just one way: to 45 degrees left. Blades function with a 7/8-inch stroke. The machine does not have an air blower and the plastic guard that pivots from the upper arm does not function too well as a hold-down. There are other, similar machines on the market, so it's possible that they are ready-made imports with particular modifica-

*Fig. 1-27.* The bottom blade clamp can pivot forward, so threading the blade through an entry hole for an internal cut is easily accomplished.

tions to suit the US from that presents it on the market. The saw, and its brothers, are not fragile because they have cast-iron substructures and tables.

## SHOPSMITH SAWS

The original Shopsmith saw (always and still called "jigsaw," even in the company's *Power Tool Woodworking for Everyone* book) has a tubular, fixed arm with a cut-width capacity of 18 inches. It was first introduced as a major accessory for the Shopsmith multipurpose tool. Used as so, it is mounted on the power-mount end of the machine and received its power and speed—infinitely variable between 700 and 1150 CS/ M—from the machine's power component that is encased in the headstock (Fig. 1-31). Later, it was offered as an individual tool for mounting with a special bracket on a steel stand or a homemade wooden one. When the tool is used alone, fit it with a motor, V-belt, and pulleys that approximate the speeds listed above.

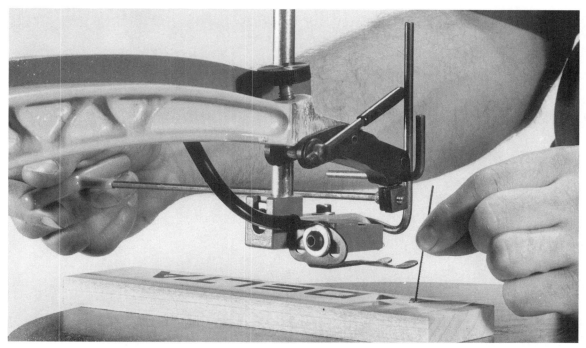

*Fig. 1-28.* After the blade is through the work, it is returned to correct position and locked in the top clamp.

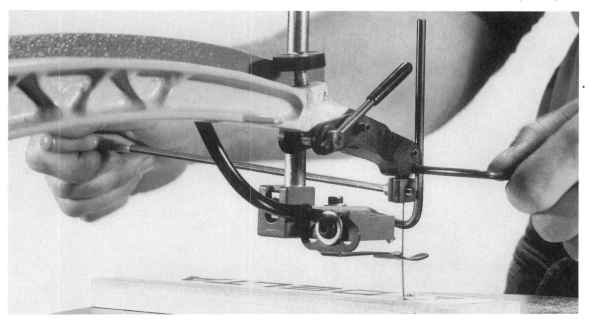

*Fig. 1-29.* A long T-wrench is used to turn the screw that brings the clamp blocks to bear against the blade. A round pin keeps the clamps in position while the T-wrench is used.

*Fig. 1-30.* Delta offers a unit that is low in price but with features that duplicate those found on more expensive tools. This can be an import, but with modifications to suit the company's standards.

The tool's lower chuck (Fig. 1-32) is designed so it can be used to grip shanked tools like machine files and sanding sticks. The chuck also can be indexed so blades can be used 90 degrees from their normal position.

The aluminum table measures 11 inches square and can be tilted one way—to the right, up to 45 degrees. The tubular arm can be removed or simply swung down out of the way when saber sawing is employed to cut oversize workpieces.

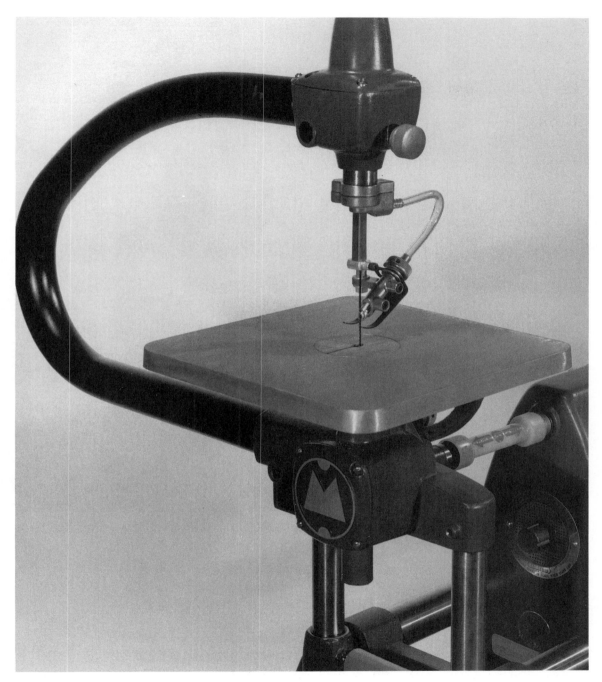

*Fig. 1-31.* The Shopsmith fixed-arm saw was originally offered for mounting on the company's multipurpose tool. Coupled to the machine, it has variable speeds of 700 to 1150 CS/M. It also can be used as an individual tool with its own motor.

*Fig. 1-32.* The tool's lower chuck will grip round shank cutters as well as saw blades. Note the under-the-table, fiber backup for the blade.

As with other tools of this type, the blade is powered on the down stroke and depends on a spring device for the return. The mechanism to accomplish this is encased in a tube that can be locked at various heights to provide blade tension (Fig. 1-33).

The Shopsmith company will not be left out when it comes to the search for the ultimate scroll saw. Its entry, one that was recently introduced, is shown in Fig. 1-34. It's a substantial machine of parallel-arm design that, like its fixed-arm predecessor, can be mounted as a major accessory for the multipurpose tool, getting power and speeds from the main tool's headstock, or as an individual tool on its own stand and with a built-in motor.

*Fig. 1-33.* The return of the blade on the Shopsmith fixed-arm saw is provided by a conventional spring-loaded plunger assembly. Other components include, air blower, blade guide and backup, and adjustable spring-type hold-down.

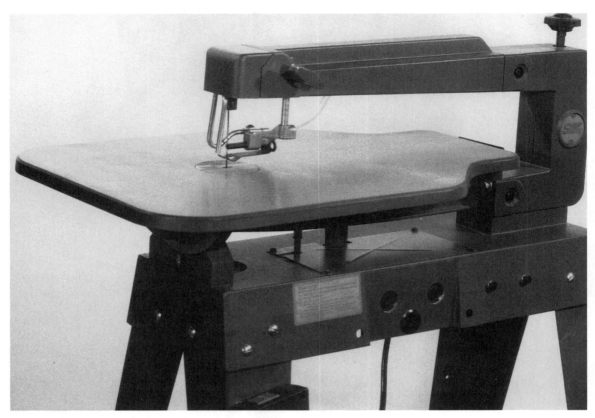

*Fig. 1-34.* Shopsmith's recently introduced, parallel-arm scroll saw, like its predecessor, can be powered by the multipurpose machine or, as shown here, with its own motor when mounted on an individual stand.

When the new machine is mounted on the Shopsmith, it operates with variable speeds of 280 to 1200 CS/M. As an individual tool, with the side-mounted control shown in Fig. 1-35, variable speeds range from 500 to 1200 CS/M. The table measures 16 inches by almost 24 inches, and it can be tilted to the left or right up to 45 degrees.

Saw blades, 5 inches long and up to 1/4 inch wide, are secured at each end with assemblies that consist of a blade holder and a blade clamp. Blades are first mounted, off the machine, in their assemblies, in a special blade-mounting fixture that is supplied with the tool (Fig. 1-36). The assembly of blade and mounting-block units is then installed in the machine with spring-loaded lock pins. The system, not exclusive with Shopsmith, is fairly new and quite practical because it provides for correct installation of the blade before it is placed in its working position.

Above-table devices include a tiltable spring hold-down, adjustable blade backup, dust blower, and a tubular guard (Fig. 1-37). A hinged arm-hood provides for access to the upper blade mounting block assembly and its lock pin.

*Fig. 1-35.* When the machine is used individually, a side-mounted control panel provides infinitely variable speeds of 500 to 1200 CS/M. The control has convenient on – off switches plus a locking device.

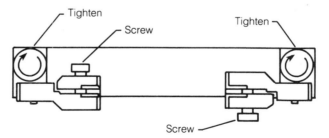

*Fig. 1-36.* The blade-mounting fixture that is supplied with the Shopsmith tool can be mounted on a wooden block for easy use. Blades are installed correctly before they are mounted in the machine.

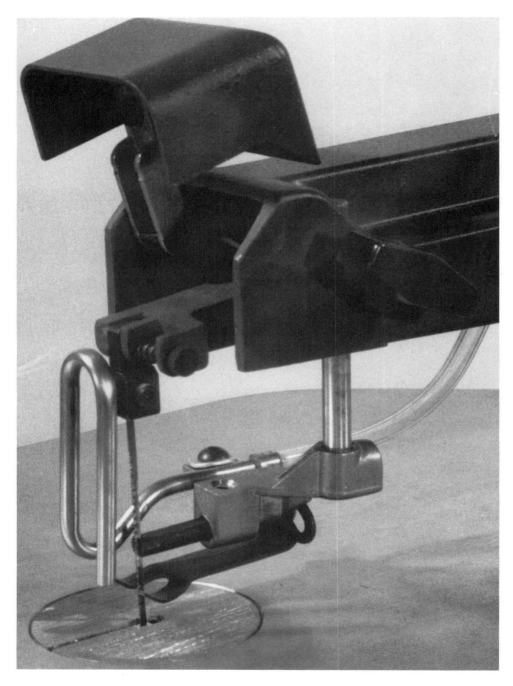

*Fig. 1-37.* Above-table devices include blade guide and backup and adjustable spring-type hold-down. Note that the tubular guard also serves to direct air that clears sawdust from around the blade.

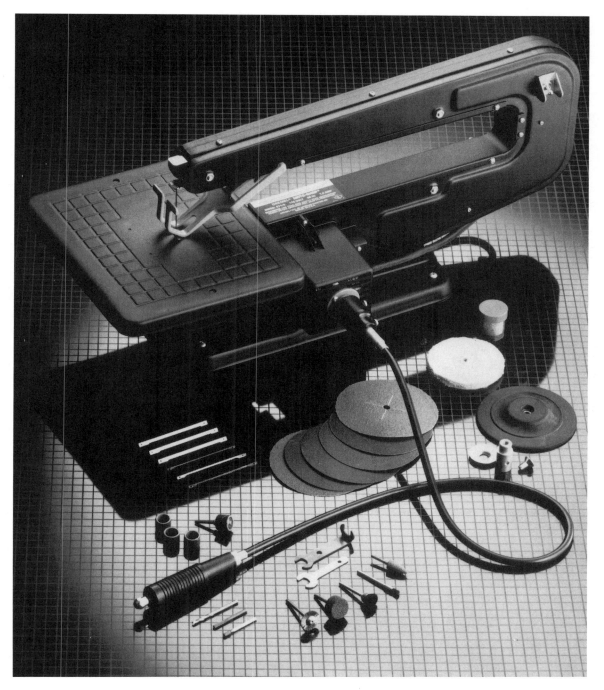

*Fig. 1-38.* The ''old'' but still alive Dremel product is listed as the ''Moto-Shop'' when it is purchased with all the accessories shown here. It is also available as a saw plus disc sander as the ''Scroll Saw/Sander.'' Buying the basic machine doesn't preclude adding other accessories.

## DREMEL PRODUCTS

The product that is shown in Fig. 1-38 which together with its accessories is called the "Moto-Shop," is a no-nonsense little machine that makes no pretense about competing with scroll saws that might weigh and cost twenty times as much. But it need make no excuses either, having been a popular tool for many years. Despite its small size, it does have a 15-inch throat. Its depth-of-cut capacity in soft wood is 1³/₄ inches; in hard woods up to ¹/₂ inch. It also can be used to saw aluminum that doesn't exceed ¹/₁₆ inch in thickness, and ³/₆₄-inch copper (18 gauge).

The Moto-Shop scroll saw operates with a direct drive motor that moves the blade at 3450 CS/M. It does have a comparatively short stroke, but many workers find this an advantage when sawing thin materials. A nice feature is an adjustment that allows the table to be raised so sawing will happen on an unused section of the blade. This will reduce the depth of cut but it is not significant when sawing veneers and other thin materials.

The table's size is 8 inches × 9¹/₂ inches and it can be tilted to the left or right up to 45 degrees. The tool operates with 3-inch, pin-type blades that are installed as shown in Figs. 1-39 and 1-40. When the tool is purchased with all its accessories, or when accessories are added, it becomes a multipurpose machine allowing, among other things, disc sanding and the use of a flexible shaft (Figs. 1-41 and 1-42).

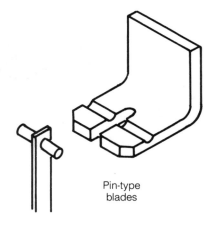

*Fig. 1-39.* The machine works with pin-type blades that situate in mounts that allow the blade's teeth to point normally, left or right, even to the rear.

Pin-type
blades

The product can be attached to a special stand or to a workbench, but it has suction cups attached to its base so it can be mounted temporarily to just about any surface—how about a patio or kitchen table?

As indicated by its new 16-inch, parallel-arm scroll saw (Fig. 1-43), the Dremel company isn't about to be left out of the current trend toward constant-tension saws. The intent of the company was to produce a respectable machine with significant features, at a reasonable price (in the area of $200). I think they have reached the goal in good style. The new tool is handsome and compact, can be mounted on its

*Fig. 1-40.* Blades are installed by passing them through the table to engage the lower mount and then hooking them to the top mount. The mount has enough spring action to facilitate placing the blade. No wrenches or other tools are needed.

*Fig. 1-41.* You are not about to sand logs on the Moto-Shop disc sander, but it is very handy for many small projects. Like other vertical circular sanders, the work is always applied to the ''down'' side of the disc.

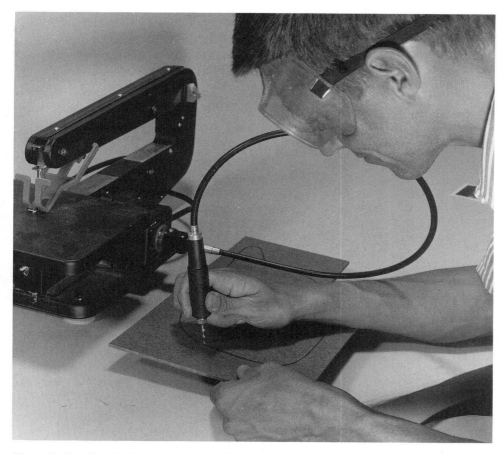

*Fig. 1-42.* The flex shaft can be used to drill entry holes that are needed when doing piercing. The shaft's handpiece also will secure a variety of small drum sanders and a variety of burrs and cutters.

own stand, which is available as an accessory (Fig. 1-44), or to an existing, sturdy surface.

A $1/10$ HP, direct drive motor that can be switched to deliver the blade's $3/4$-inch stroke at either a slow speed of 890 or high speed of 1790 CS/M, is built in. Its 12-inch round, aluminum table can be tilted up to 45 degrees. At this table setting, the tool's normal 2-inch depth of cut is reduced to 1 inch. The basic machine has mounts for 5 inch, pin-type blades that can be installed for normal cutting, or situated for rip-cutting on workpieces that are longer than 16 inches. Also, pivoting blade adapters that allow the use of 5-inch plain-end blades, are available accessories.

A nice touch is the blade adapter gauges that are attached to the cover of the top arm (Figs. 1-45 and 1-46). These allow the correct assembly of blade and blade

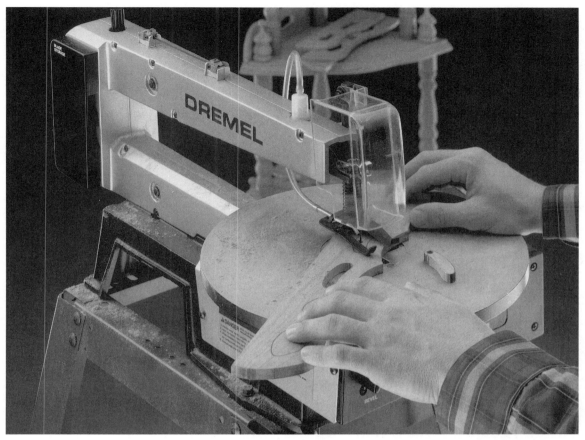

*Fig. 1-43.* Dremel has just introduced a low-cost, parallel-arm scroll saw that is handsome and compact and that will function with pin-type blades or with accessory mounts that take plain-end blades. A box at the rear of the tool will store blades and extra blade mounts.

holders before they are mounted in the arms. Extra blade adapters make sense because the user can have an assortment of ready-to-mount blades always on hand. The adapters are designed so blades can be used normally or 90 degrees from the head-on position.

A bellows-type blower that pushes air through a tube that is attached to the hold-down feet, does a good job of removing sawdust from the cut line (Fig. 1-47).

## HEGNER SAWS

The name Hegner is as familiar to scroll saw operators as, for example, Apple or IBM are to people involved with computers. Hegner machines have, and continue to, set standards. Many of Hegner's practical innovations have been adopted by competitive organizations. It is said, and probably justifiably, that Hegner products are signifi-

*Fig. 1-44.* The new Dremel saw can be mounted on a steel stand that is offered by the company or to an existing work surface. Like all scroll saws, any mounting arrangement should provide for minimum vibration.

cantly responsible for the current, general interest in scroll sawing. Among the features of Hegner saws is the patented blade suspension system that, roughly, involves V-shaped blade clamps that sit and pivot in matching configurations on the ends of the arms. This, plus a drive system that produces a fully articulating parallelogram, provides for powering the blade on both up and down strokes in a manner that ensures the blade will be constantly vertical. Simply, in practice, it means that the cut will always be square to adjacent surfaces.

The most recent member of the Hegner family, designated as Multimax-18, is shown in Fig. 1-48. The "18" in the name tells the tool's width-of-cut capacity. This

*Fig. 1-45.* The Dremel saw being used for a piercing operation. Note the blade adapter gauges that are attached to the cover of the upper arm.

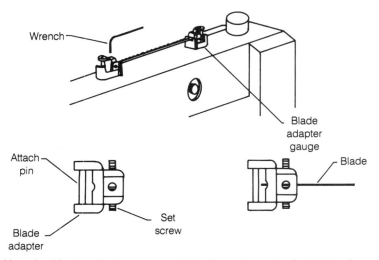

Wrench

Blade adapter gauge

Attach pin

Blade adapter

Set screw

Blade

*Fig. 1-46.* How the blade adapters are used. Having extra sets of adapters is a good idea because you can have an assortment of ready-mounted blades on hand.

*Fig. 1-47.* The air blower does a good job of keeping the cutline clear of sawdust. The air nozzle moves vertically together with the spring-type hold-down.

machine can saw stock up to $2^5/8$ inches thick, a depth-of-cut capacity that is tough to match in the scroll-saw field, but even the supplier (Advanced Machinery Imports, LTD) suggests that this be reduced to 2 inches when sawing very dense materials, such as hard maple and birch. Sawing in thicker pieces of these and similar species can be done, but there will be a noticeable decrease in sawing speed.

The table, with dimensions of 9 inches × about 17 inches, can be tilted up to 45 degrees to the left and to a maximum of 15 degrees to the right. The unit is available with a 2.8 amp motor and integral speed control that delivers 400 to 1500 CS/M (Figs. 1-49 and 1-50), or with a 1.9 amp motor that provides a single speed of 1660 CS/M. The blade stroke equals about $7/8$ inch.

Figure 1-51 shows the blade clamp in position on the upper arm of the tool. The spring-loaded knob above the clamp is adjusted for a gap between its end and the top of the blade clamp. This is necessary so the triangular blade clamp can pivot

*Fig. 1-48.* The Multimax-18 is the latest member of the Hegner scroll-saw family. Like its relatives, it incorporates many of the features that have made Hegner a respected name in this area of tools.

freely. The hold-down is a steel component with a front-mounted "guard" that is adjustable vertically, and that can be swung out of the way. The hold-down, because it is attached to its own arm, can be removed from the machine if the operator chooses to work without it.

If you wonder why there is an accordion-type spring on the rear of some scroll saws (Fig. 1-52) it's a safety device that's meant to immediately stop the movement of the upper arm should a blade snap during sawing.

Hegner has an array of scroll saws in varied sizes and price ranges. What follows is a brief run down on what they offer. I suggest that readers who are interested in more detailed information drop a line to AMI LTD, P.O. Box 312, New Castle, DE 19720. Tell them that Cris sent you.

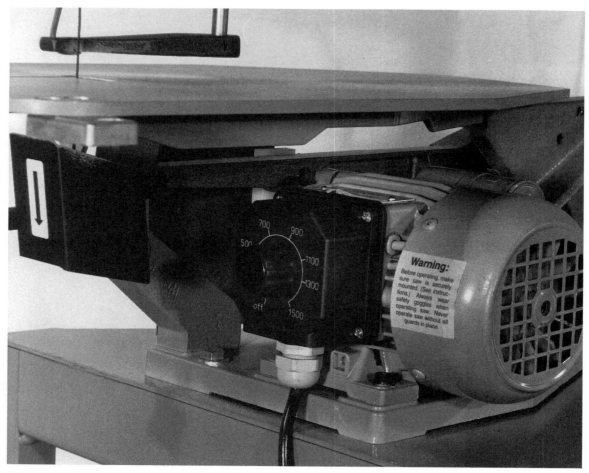

*Fig. 1-49.* The new unit is available with an integral speed control that provides 400 to 1500 CS/M, or with a single speed of 1660 CS/M. You buy it one way or the other. The variable speed control is not for customer installation.

MULTIMAX-3 has a generous 25-inch throat and a 10-inch × 20 1/2-inch table. It can be fitted for a single speed of 1660 CS/M or a control that provides variable speeds. Stroke length can be either 3/8 inch or 7/8 inch; maximum cut depth is better than 2 inches.

The MULTIMAX-2 has a 9-inch × 17-inch table and a throat capacity of 14 3/8 inches. It was a forerunner of the new generation of constant-tension scroll saws and, with time-proven improvements, is still going strong. The blade's stroke is 7/8 inch and the motor provides it with 1660 CS/M. A variable speed feature is available as an accessory.

## Blade selection

| Material | Thickness mm | Recommended blades Length 130 mm |
|---|---|---|
| Wood | ... 5<br>5 ... 30<br>30 ... 50 | Pebeco n° 1<br>Pebeco n° 5<br>Pebeco n° 9<br>Gottfried 130×2.5×0.55 |
| Aluminum<br>Soft brass<br>Soft copper,<br>etc. | ... 3<br>3 ... 12 | Pebeco n° 1<br>Pebeco n° 5<br>Gottfried 130×2.5×0.55 |
| Steel<br>Hard brass<br>Hard copper,<br>etc. | ... 1<br>1 ... 3<br>3 ... 5<br>5 ... 12 | Goldsnail n° 1<br>Goldsnail n° 5<br>Goldsnail n° 9<br>Goldsnail n° 12 |
| Plastics | ... 2<br>2 ... 30<br>10 ... 50 | Pebeco n° 1<br>Pebeco n° 5, n° 9<br>Gottfried 130×2.5×0.55 |

*Fig. 1-50.* A handy chart attached to the machine suggests the right blade for various materials and thicknesses. The names of the blades are peculiar to those supplied by Hegner.

The HOBBYMAX is the least expensive of Hegner saws, but that does not indicate a decrease in quality. Its C-arm structure has a 14-inch throat; table size is $6\frac{1}{2}$ × 12 inches. Blade stroke is short—$3/8$ inch, but its cut capacity, at 1560 CS/M is 1 inch in either hard or soft wood. It also can handle metals as thick as $3/16$ inch and plastics up to $3/8$ inch. It might seem "small" compared to other Hegner units, but it's no baby. It's a nice, precision tool that can easily turn out projects, such as the coach model that is shown in Fig. 1-53.

### A SAW WITH A "WALKING BEAM"

The Craftsman (Sears) "walking beam" saw that is shown in Figs. 1-54 and 1-55 is its own breed of scroll saw in that it has a couple of exclusive and practical features that are not duplicated elsewhere. A major departure from conventional design is the way bevel sawing is accomplished. The entire working unit can be rotated 45 degrees to left or right in a semicircular configuration that is part of the base casting. Thus, the blade tilts to a necessary angle while the table remains horizontal (Fig. 1-56). The table has grooves at right angles to each other so that a supplied miter gauge can be used for guiding crosscuts or cross bevels (Fig. 1-57), and, when locked so its head is parallel to the saw blade, can be used as a rip fence. Guided cuts are not the norm on scroll saws, but with a proper blade in prime condition, and careful feeding of the work, results can be acceptable, especially if a wide blade is used.

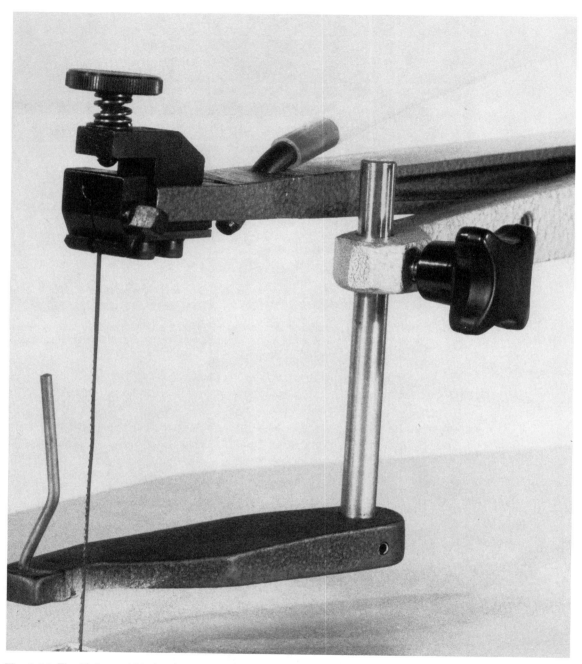

*Fig. 1-51.* The V-shaped blade clamps suit the configuration of the blade mounts. The upper knob is set for a space between its end and the blade clamp so that the blade clamp can move through its pivoting action.

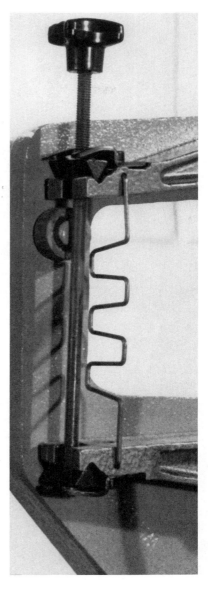

*Fig. 1-52.* The accordion spring at the rear of the tool's structure stops the movement of the upper arm should a blade break during sawing. The vertical rod is the machine's tensioning device.

The table also is cast with pockets that hold the tool's blade clamps while blades are installed. It's a way of ensuring precise mounting before the blade is installed in the arms (Fig. 1-58).

Despite what it is called, the design is basically that of a parallel-arm, constant-tension saw. The throat size is 18 inches; maximum cut is 2 inches, but this reduces to 1$^1$/$_8$ inches when cutting is done at 45 degrees. The unit can be used with plain-end blades either 5 or 6 inches long, and it will also accept 5-inch pin-type blades. The blade clamps, in combination with the mounting arrangement in the arms, allow

*Fig. 1-53.* This coach model was supplied by Hegner as an example of what can be done with its Hobbymax product, the least expensive of Hegner saws.

*Fig. 1-54.* The Craftsman (Sears) "walking beam" scroll saw is essentially a parallel-arm, constant-tension machine. Heavy bumpers are provided to minimize vibration when the tool is mounted on a wooden stand.

*Fig. 1-55.* The tool's combination guard and hold-down pivots are on the cover of the upper arm. Hold-down action is possible because the guard can be locked at various altitudes in relation to the thickness of the stock.

the blade to be situated 90 degrees from its normal position when long rip-type cuts are needed. A rear-mounted, direct-drive motor delivers 1600 CS/M; length of blade stroke is $7/8$ inch. The die-cast aluminum table has dimensions of 9 inches $\times$ 14$3/8$ inches.

The Sears '89 catalog also lists an imported, 16-inch conventional-design scroll saw with a tilting table that allows a normal 2-inch cut and a 1-inch cut at 45 degrees. A direct-drive motor supplies 1700 CS/M. Also listed in the Sears catalog is the small Dremel saw with its accessories.

*Fig. 1-56.* The entire upper structure of the machine can be rotated left or right in a semicircular cavity that is part of the base casting. Thus, for bevel cutting, the table remains in a horizontal position.

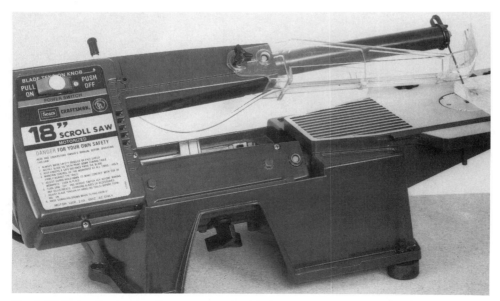

*Fig. 1-57.* Using the tool's miter gauge as a guide for a crossbevel operation. Careful feeding and the proper blade are required for guided cuts to be as accurate as you might like.

*Fig. 1-58.* Intersecting grooves allow the miter gauge to be used for crosscutting and ripping. Note the cast blade-holder pockets in the table. Using them to install blades in their clamps ensures correct installation before blades are placed in the machine.

*Fig. 1-59.* AMT's 16-inch scroll saw has many "big name" features, yet is quite low in price. It is a sturdy tool with a direct-drive motor that moves the blade at 1725 CS/M.

## FROM AMT

The American Machine & Tool Company's scroll-saw offering, shown in Fig. 1-59, fits the description of being a sturdy, low cost machine with many of the features found on more expensive tools. The 16-inch throat machine has a 2-inch depth of cut and provides constant tension through a parallel-arm design. Although the tool is initially supplied with holders for 5-inch, pin-type blades (Fig. 1-60), accessory blade clamps and user-installed mounts permit the use of plain-end blades with a pivoting action that is similar to what is found on higher priced units. A direct-drive motor moves the blade, with its ³/₄-inch stroke, at 1725 CS/M. The 8-inch × almost 15-inch table tilts one way—left to 45 degrees. A pivoting blade guard (Fig. 1-61), snaps into place on

*Fig. 1-60.* The tool is organized with holders for pin-type blades, but an economical accessory kit allows the use of plain-end blades that will function with the pivoting action that is boasted of on higher-priced tools.

the cover of the upper arm. A little, piston-type unit that is activated by the movement of the upper arm, delivers air to clear away sawdust from the cut line (Fig. 1-62). The nozzle can be positioned to direct air to pertinent areas. A nice touch, one found on some other scroll saws, is a switch key that must be installed before the tool can be turned on. Removal of the key prevents unauthorized use.

**Fig. 1-61.** The blade guard hooks into place on the cover of the upper arm. The guard, because it has an easy pivot action, does not function too well as a hold-down.

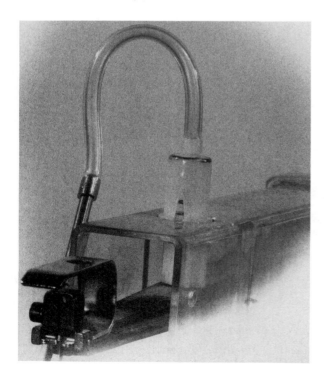

**Fig. 1-62.** Piston-type air supplier is activated by the movement of the upper arm. The air nozzle can be situated for most efficient removal of sawdust.

# Chapter 2

# Scroll Saw Blades

**T**HERE ARE ARMIES OF SCROLL SAW BLADES, TO THE POINT WHERE THERE CAN BE UNDER-standable confusion among people just starting with scroll-saw operations. There are differences in thickness, width, teeth per inch (TPI), lengths, and styles. Each blade, under particular conditions, can do the best job. While there are many suggestions and recommendations, in the final analysis, it is the operator who must judge what blade will produce the results he seeks. Many workers, including pros, will as I do, "play" with a blade, randomly making cuts in a small or scrap piece of the material to be sawed (Fig. 2-1). The trial system also leads to discovery of the best speed and feed pressure (how fast you try to move the work) to use. It isn't necessary to start "blind." Be guided by the listings in Tables 2-1 and 2-2 to start with, then make changes as you feel they are needed. Keep a log of results so you can quickly organize for duplicate operations. The method also contributes to economical use of blades. Even though they are reasonably priced, there is little point in getting less from them than you should.

## TYPES

Blades are identified by their physical dimensions—thickness, width, and teeth per inch, as shown in Fig. 2-2. Many suppliers are now using identification numbers (generic), each number identifying a blade of particular physical makeup. The wider and thicker the blade, the coarser and wider the kerf will be (Fig. 2-3). A general consideration for scroll sawing is to use the widest that will produce the results you want.

*Fig. 2-1.* Experimenting with a blade you are not familiar with by making random cuts in the material that will be used for the project is a good way to become acquainted with the blade's characteristics.

Blades are either "plain end" or "pin type," with plain-end blades being the most prevalent because they are used in most scroll saws (Fig. 2-4). Plain-end blades are gripped between blade clamps that vary in design depending on the saw, while pin-type blades commonly rest in grooved blade mounts that are similar to what is shown in Fig. 2-5.

Regardless of what blade is used or how it is mounted, it always must be installed so that the points of its teeth point down toward the table (Fig. 2-6). If the blade is mounted in a reverse fashion, each up stroke would lift the work from the table so it would be difficult to control. Many blades are so fine, it's difficult to visually determine the direction of the teeth. A magnifying glass will help, or you can determine tooth-point direction by *very* lightly running a fingertip along the blade's cutting edge. A smooth passage will mean that you are moving your finger in the direction the teeth are pointing.

Another consideration that applies to all blades is that the TPI should be such that, ideally, at least three teeth make contact with the edge of the workpiece (Fig. 2-7). This is especially important when sawing tougher materials, such as ferrous and nonferrous metals.

## Table 2-1. The Blades Listed in the Delta Catalog.

### Conventional Blades

| Size | | Delta Cat. Number | Materials To Use On |
|---|---|---|---|
| Width | TPI | | |
| .070 | 32 | 40 – 058 | Aluminum - Copper - Lead - Iron - Steel Iron |
| .070 | 20 | 40 – 159 | Felt - Paper - Asbestos - Pewter |
| .070 | 15 | 40 – 160 | Brass - Copper - Lead - Iron - Steel |
| .085 | 15 | 40 – 161 | Asbestos - Pewter - Aluminum |
| .110 | 20 | 40 – 164 | Wood |
| .250 | 20 | 40 – 165 | Pewter - Aluminum - Brass - Brake Lining - Mica - Copper - Steel - Iron |
| .035 | 20 | 40 – 184 | Very Thin Materials - Veneers - Plastics - Ivory - Bakelite - Hard Rubber |
| .050 | 15 | 40 – 185 | Plastics - Celluloid |
| .070 | 7 | 40 – 187 | Bakelite |
| .110 | 7 | 40 – 188 | Wood - Ivory |
| .110 | 15 | 40 – 191 | Wood - Pressed Wood - Bone - Felt - Copper - Ivory - Aluminum - Wall Board - Paper - Lead |
| .110 | 10 | 40 – 192 | |
| .187 | 10 | 40 – 193 | Hard and Soft Woods |
| .250 | 7 | 40 – 194 | |
| .054 | 30 | 40 – 195 | Pewter - Mica - Pearl |
| .054 | 20 | 40 – 196 | Sea Shells - Pressed Wood |
| .085 | 12 | 40 – 198 | Hard Leather |

(Courtesy Delta International)

## SKIP-TOOTH BLADES

Skip-tooth blades, shown compared with a conventional blade in Fig. 2-8, have an open area between teeth. Actually, the blade is manufactured so that alternate teeth are eliminated. The design is meant to provide a cooler cutting, faster blade action, and more efficient sawdust clearance from the kerf. Another skip-tooth design has

## Table 2-2. Shopsmith Assortment with Suggestions for Best Speed to Use.

| Blade | | | | Minimum Radius | SPM* | Applications |
|---|---|---|---|---|---|---|
| SS # | TPI | Kerf | Width | | | |
| 555265 | 9** | .030 | .100 | 1/8 | 500 – 1200 | Plywood, Plastic, Hard and Soft Wood (1/4″ to 2″) |
| 555261 | 9 1/2 | .024 | .062 | 3/32 | 500 – 720 | Plywood, Plastic, Paper, Felt, Bone, |
| 55562 | 11 1/2 | .018 | .053 | 1/16 | 500 – 930 | Hard and Soft Wood—(1/8″ to 1 1/4″ for 555261, and 1/16″ to 1″ for 555262) |
| 555263 | 12 1/2 | .016 | .038 | 3/64 | 500 – 1130 | Horn, Paper, Bone, Plastic, Plywood, Hard and Soft Wood |
| 555264 | 20 | .012 | .029 | 1/32 | 500 – 1200 | Mother-of-Pearl, Ivory, Plastic, Bone, Fiber, Veneer, Hard and Soft Wood |
| 505767 | 57 | .010 | .021 | 1/64 | 500 – 650 | Nonferrous Metals, Mother-of-pearl, Bone, |
| 505766 | 65 | .009 | .017 | 1/64 | 500 – 560 | Fiber, Ivory, Plastic, Veneer, Hard |
| 505765 | 80 | .007 | .014 | 1/64 | 500 – 530 | and Soft Wood |

\* .... Strokes per minute
\*\* .... With three reverse teeth

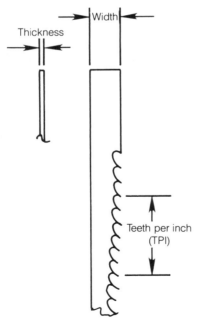

*Fig. 2-2.* Scroll saw blades are identified by their physical dimensions and the number of teeth per inch.

Blade nomenclature

*Fig. 2-3.* The wider and thicker the blade, the greater will be the kerf that is formed. Generally, it's good practice to work with the widest blade that will produce the results you seek.

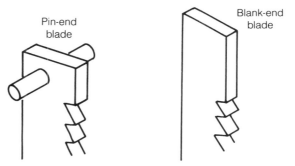

*Fig. 2-4.* Blades have blank- or pin-type ends. Some machines take only one type; others will accommodate either design.

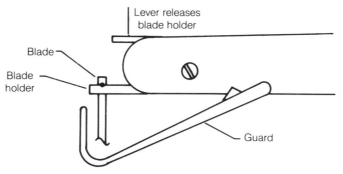

*Fig. 2-5.* Pin-type blades sit in mounts that are grooved for the pins. The grooves commonly allow the blade to point in any of four directions.

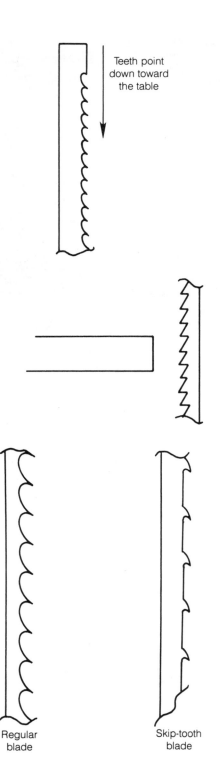

Teeth point
down toward
the table

*Fig. 2-6.* Blades must be mounted so the teeth point down toward the table.

*Fig. 2-7.* Blades will function better and will have a longer life if they are chosen so that at least three teeth make contact with the edge of the workpiece.

*Fig. 2-8.* Regular skip-tooth blades have open spaces between teeth. They are made so alternate teeth are eliminated.

Regular
blade

Skip-tooth
blade

## Table 2-3. Skip-tooth Blades Offered
## by the Olson Saw Company. Note the Identification Numbers.

| Skip-Tooth Blades | | | | |
|---|---|---|---|---|
| Size | | | # | Applications |
| Width | Thick. | TPI | | |
| .067 | .020 | 9.5 | 12 | A set of blades to have on hand for gen- |
| .063 | .019 | 9.5 | 11 | eral sawing—they can be used effi- |
| .059 | .019 | 11 | 10 | ciently on soft and hard wood in a |
| .053 | .018 | 11.5 | 9 | thickness range of about 3/16″ to 2″— |
| .047 | .017 | 11.5 | 8 | also good for materials, such as plastics |
| .043 | .016 | 12 | 7 | and bone |
| .040 | .016 | 13 | 6 | For tight radii in materials thicker than |
| .037 | .015 | 14 | 5 | 1/8″—good for all woods and nonwood materials, such as horn, bone, and plastics |
| .033 | .014 | 15 | 4 | Choose blades of this size for tight work |
| .032 | .013 | 18 | 3 | in thin materials (about 3/32″ to 1/8″)— |
| .029 | .012 | 20 | 2 | wood and veneers, plastics, ivory, etc. |
| .025 | .011 | 23 | 1 | Blades of this size are excellent for intri- |
| .024 | .011 | 25 | 0 | cate sawing in materials from about |
| .022 | .010 | 28 | 2/0 | 1/16″ to 3/32″—use on veneers, plastics, pearl, hard rubber, and more |

sets of two teeth with open areas between them. Many people who are engaged in marquetry recommend using the double tooth blade for that type of veneer sawing. Typical offerings in regular skip-tooth blade designs, together with suggested applications, are listed in Table 2-3.

## BLADES WITH REVERSE TEETH

The name reverse teeth doesn't mean that all teeth point in a nonnormal manner—only that a set of teeth at the bottom edge of the blade are filed opposite to the direction of conventional ones (Fig. 2-9). The purpose of the design is to minimize the splintering or feathering that occurs when a regular blade leaves the bottom surface of the workpiece. It's a nice idea but might not work on all machines because the reverse tooth area is limited and, because of blade stroke and table position, might not make it above the tool's table surface. If all the special teeth do is stroke *under* the table, then they don't come into play. The people at the Olson Saw Company, who supply the blades, have advised of their awareness of the problem and will produce

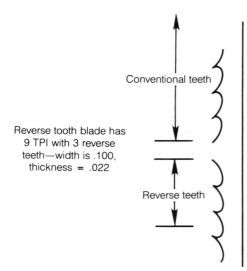

Conventional teeth

Reverse tooth blade has
9 TPI with 3 reverse
teeth—width is .100,
thickness = .022

Reverse teeth

*Fig. 2-9.* Reverse tooth blades
have a limited number of teeth at
the bottom end that point in a
direction opposite to that of conventional teeth.

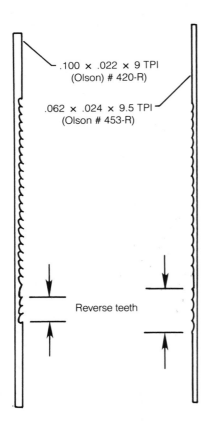

.100 × .022 × 9 TPI
(Olson) # 420-R)

.062 × .024 × 9.5 TPI
(Olson # 453-R)

Reverse teeth

*Fig. 2-10.* Examples of reverse
tooth blades.

this style of blade (probably available by the time this book is published) with a greater number of reverse teeth. Examples of reverse-tooth blades that could be purchased at the time of this writing are illustrated in Fig. 2-10.

## SPIRAL BLADES

If you have ever used a *drill saw*, the type of cutter that can be used in a portable drill to saw, actually *rasp*, in any direction, you will have an idea of how spiral blades work, but not about how they are made. Drill saws are rods with peripheral cutting points—spiral blades are actually of standard size and tooth configuration, but they are physically twisted so teeth point in all directions. What this means, when such blades are used on a scroll saw, is that you can make "spot" turns in any direction without having to rotate the work to keep the blade on the cutting line as you must when using conventional blades. The difference between the two programs is demonstrated in Figs. 2-11 and 2-12.

Two factors to consider about spiral blades are that the larger they are the more sawdust they will move up to the surface of the work, and, because they cut in all directions, it requires more control to prevent the blade from following grain lines instead of pattern lines. It is important, upon introduction, that the user experiment with tension, speed, and work handling to become acquainted with the sawing characteristics of the blade design. An exclusive application for spiral blades is a type of

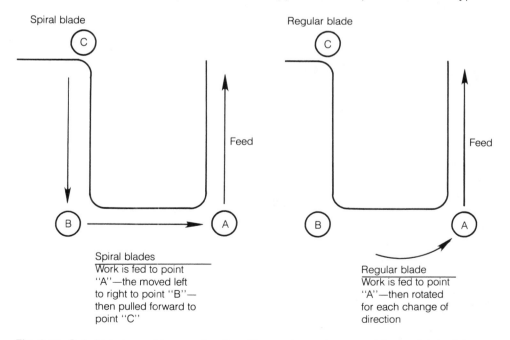

Spiral blades
Work is fed to point "A"—the moved left to right to point "B"—then pulled forward to point "C"

Regular blade
Work is fed to point "A"—then rotated for each change of direction

*Fig. 2-11.* Spiral blades cut in any direction. The work can be moved forward, left, right, or backward. With a regular blade, the work must be rotated to keep the blade on the pattern line.

*Fig. 2-12.* With a spiral blade you can easily pull back work to remove the blade from the kerf.

bevel sawing that results, for example, in letters or numbers that slant only in one direction. The technique, which can't be accomplished with conventional blades, will be demonstrated in chapter 7.

Spiral blades are available in various sizes, with different kerf widths, so you can, within limits, choose one that is right for the job (Fig. 2-13). This type of blade is recognized by kerf width and TPI. Those that are listed in Table 2-4, together with identification numbers, are offered by the Olson Saw Company, the developer of the design.

## JEWELERS BLADES

The material used for jewelers blades is hardened and tempered steel. These blades are primarily recommended for sawing metal and other hardened materials. They

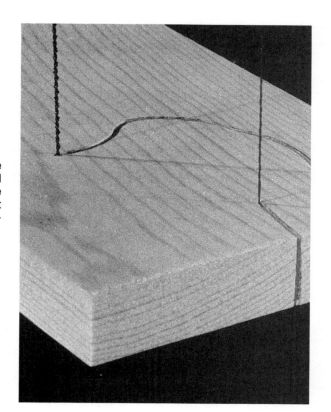

*Fig. 2-13.* Spiral blades continue to cut regardless of work-feed direction. Some fine ones are available but the smallest won't cut as fine a kerf as some conventional blades.

**Table 2-4. Spiral Blade Sizes. Note that only kerf width and TPI are needed to tell the size of the blade.**

| Spiral Blades | | |
|---|---|---|
| Size | | |
| Kerf | TPI | # |
| .025 | 51 | 2/0 |
| .026 | 46 | 0 |
| .030 | 46 | 1 |
| .032 | 41 | 2 |
| .035 | 41 | 3 |
| .038 | 36 | 4 |
| .044 | 36 | 5 |
| .049 | 30 | 6 |

(Courtesy Olson Saw Co.)

have conventional saw teeth, some so fine and close together that they can easily clog when used for wood sawing, so experienced operators don't rely on them too much for general scroll work. This type of blade falls into two categories, those recommended for use in hand-held frames, and others that also can be used efficiently in powered scroll saws. Tables 2-5 and 2-6 list the blades that are available in both areas.

### Table 2-5. Metal Piercing Jewelers Blades.

| Width | Thickness | TPI | Identification # (Generic) |
|-------|-----------|-----|----------------------------|
| .022 | .011 | 51 | 0 |
| .024 | .012 | 48 | 1 |
| .028 | .013 | 43 | 2 |
| .030 | .014 | 41 | 3 |
| .031 | .015 | 38 | 4 |
| .033 | .016 | 36 | 5 |
| .038 | .017 | 33 | 6 |
| .041 | .019 | 30 | 7 |
| .049 | .022 | 25 | 9 |
| .057 | .024 | 20 | 11 |
| .070 | .023 | 20 | 12 |

### Table 2-6. Jewelers Blades Recommended for Use Only in Hand Frames.

| Width | Thickness | TPI | Identification # (Generic) |
|-------|-----------|-----|----------------------------|
| .012 | .006 | 84 | 8/0 |
| .013 | .006 | 81 | 7/0 |
| .014 | .007 | 79 | 6/0 |
| .016 | .008 | 74 | 5/0 |
| .017 | .009 | 66 | 4/0 |
| .019 | .0095 | 61 | 3/0 |
| .020 | .010 | 56 | 2/0 |
| .022 | .011 | 51 | 0 |

### SABER SAWS

There is no specific category of blades that are designed for saber-saw operations on a scroll saw. Those that have the name are supplied for use in portable tools, called *jigsaws*, like the unit shown in Fig. 2-14. The blades are comparatively short,

*Fig. 2-14.* Saber saw blades are meant to be used in this portable jigsaw. The blades can be used in scroll saws, but under conditions that do not apply to all machines.

and rigid enough so that they can function even when gripped only at one end. That's another catch as far as scroll saws are concerned. The design of the bottom blade holder of the machine must accommodate the blade without a pivot action. This kind of holder; a type of chuck is what it really is, is usually found on fixed-arm

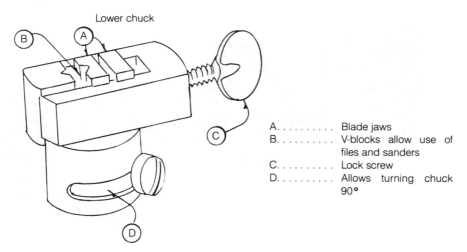

Lower chuck

A. . . . . . . . . Blade jaws
B. . . . . . . . . V-blocks allow use of files and sanders
C. . . . . . . . . Lock screw
D. . . . . . . . . Allows turning chuck 90°

*Fig. 2-15.* The kind of lower blade holder that makes it possible to utilize saber saws in a scroll saw. The design, or something similar, is usually found on fixed-arm machines.

*Fig. 2-16.* This type of saber saw blade, that can function in some scroll saws, has tungsten carbide cutting edges that can cut through tough materials, and brittle materials like ceramic tile.

tools. The bottom blade holder on the fixed-arm Delta saw, shown in Fig. 2-15, is an example. With such a design, some of the heavier scroll saw blades can be used for saber sawing.

Saber saw blades have conventional tooth configurations and while they vary in style and TPI, none can be used for the intricate sawing that is possible with regular scroll saw blades. An interesting offering in the saber saw blade area is shown in Fig. 2-16. Cutting edges are bonded with hundreds of particles of tungsten carbide so they can be used to saw, among other things, materials like ceramic tile. Chapter 9 will probe more deeply into the possibilities of saber sawing.

## BLADE STORAGE

Chances are that as you progress with scroll sawing you will accumulate an extensive assortment of blades. Keeping them in their original wire-wrapped bundles, usually in quantities of 12, as they are supplied by many manufacturers, isn't too efficient because individual blades are difficult to remove and returning one is a lost cause. It's better to supply a storage unit of some sort so the blades can be unwrapped and held safely and separate from each other.

There are many options. The ideas that are illustrated and detailed in Figs. 2-17 through 2-19 are simple to make and can be kept close to the machine with a "small" quantity of blades that are suitable for the work in progress. More elaborate projects are suggested in Figs. 2-20 through 2-23.

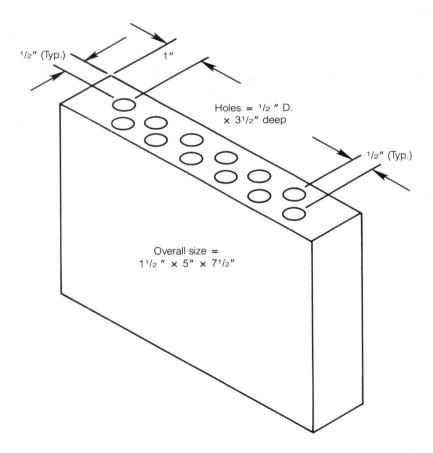

*Fig. 2-17.* A block of wood with holes for blades is an acceptable storage unit. For more blades, use a longer or thicker block and additional holes.

*Fig. 2-18.* A blade holder like this is easily made on a table saw. Kerfs ¹/₈ inch wide will accommodate any scroll saw blade.

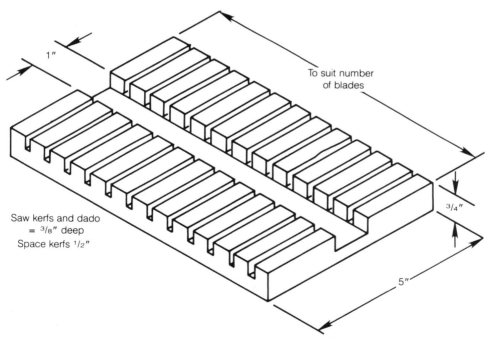

1"

To suit number
of blades

³/₄"

Saw kerfs and dado
= ³/₈" deep
Space kerfs ¹/₂"

5"

*Fig. 2-19.* The holder is easy to make on a table saw; kerfs for the blades, a wide, central dado so fingers can pick out the blade that is needed.

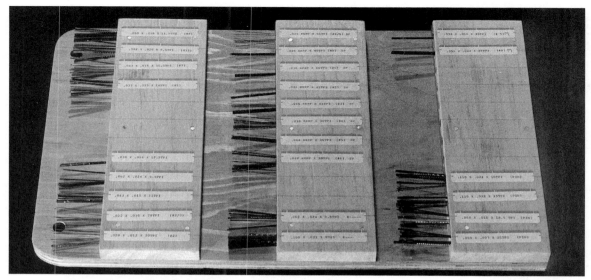

*Fig. 2-20.* This storage unit will hold 36 blade styles. Multiply by 12, which is the usual purchase quantity, and you look at 432 blades. A lot? Not really, for anyone interested in an in-depth appreciation of the scroll saw. Self-adhesive labels are used to identify the blades.

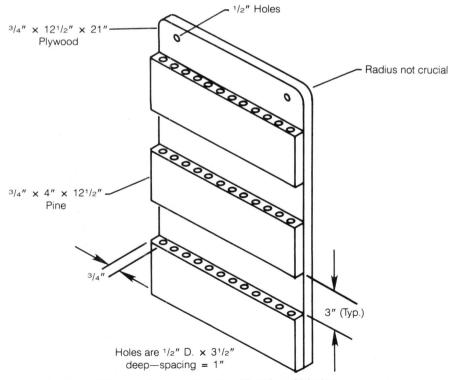

1/2" Holes

3/4" × 12 1/2" × 21"
Plywood

Radius not crucial

3/4" × 4" × 12 1/2"
Pine

3/4"

3" (Typ.)

Holes are 1/2" D. × 3 1/2"
deep—spacing = 1"

*Fig. 2-21.* How to make the unit that can be used to store 36 styles of blades.

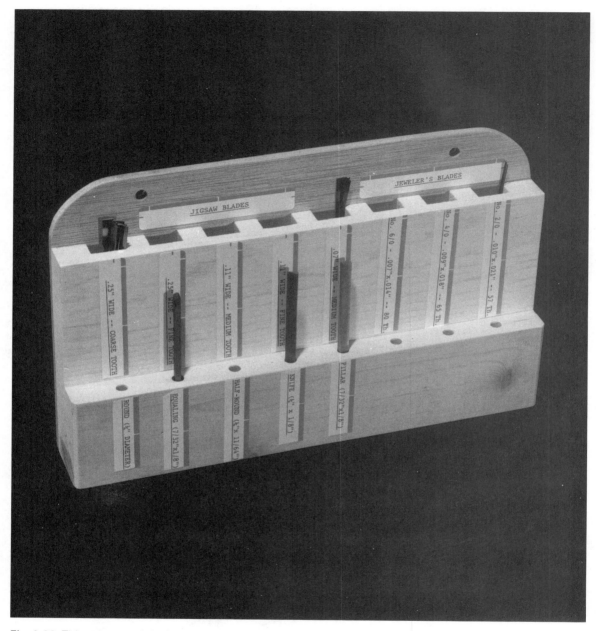

*Fig. 2-22.* This storage unit is designed to hold machine files as well as saw blades. Here too, labels are used to identify the various cutters.

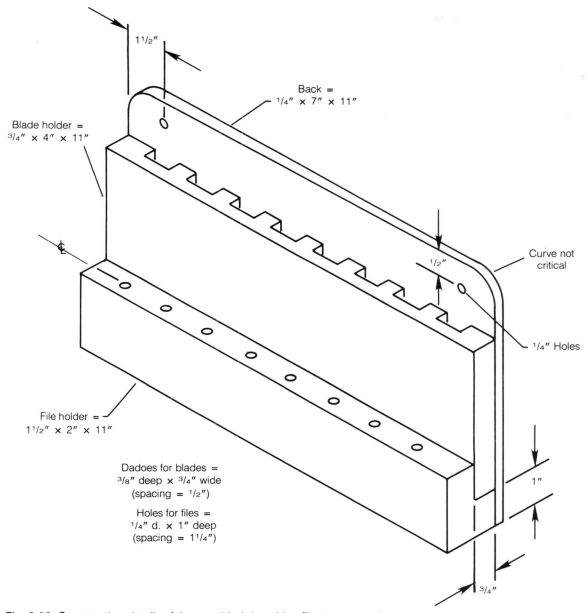

1 1/2"

Back =
1/4" × 7" × 11"

Blade holder =
3/4" × 4" × 11"

Curve not
critical

1/2"

1/4" Holes

File holder =
1 1/2" × 2" × 11"

Dadoes for blades =
3/8" deep × 3/4" wide
(spacing = 1/2")

Holes for files =
1/4" d. × 1" deep
(spacing = 1 1/4")

1"

3/4"

*Fig. 2-23.* Construction details of the saw blade/machine file storage rack.

# Chapter 3

# Safety Sense

**A** POWER TOOL DOES NOT HAVE INTELLIGENCE, NOR IS IT EQUIPPED WITH SENSORS THAT recognize what it should or should not cut. If you accept that the machine is disinterested in what you place in the path of its cutting component, you are aware of the major factor of safety sense.

Too often, a person involved in a power tool accident looks back at the occasion and asks, "Why did I do that?" Chances are that the situation was caused simply by carelessness or a feeling of immunity, an unrealistic state that does not exist for any of us. Safety rules, as they apply specifically to a tool or to general workshop activities, are often passed over because of eagerness to get to using the machine. It's not good practice, because knowing safety rules and obeying them is even more important than gaining proficiency with the tool. It doesn't make sense to be an expert with damaged fingers.

If you feel that a chapter on safety is a bore, you're in trouble right off. An important statistic proves that expertise doesn't guarantee safety. As many professionals as amateurs have accidents because they become too confident, which creates a dangerous state of mind. Generally, a beginner will have a degree of fear of the tool. This creates respect that should never be lost.

## THE TOOL

Let's agree right off that the scroll saw is not a "safe" machine. Potential accidents might be much less severe than those that can happen on, say, a table or radial arm saw, but safety sense says they should not happen at all. The first step is to conduct an in-depth study of the tool—before you use it—learning what it can do and its limitations. Because scroll saws differ in size and shape, in the way adjustments are made, and in the mechanism that drives the saw blade, it's important to accept the owner's manual that is supplied with the tool as bible, because its information will be specific.

The difference between how fixed-arm and C-arm or parallel-arm tools work has a bearing on safe finger placement (Figs. 3-1 and 3-2). When the machine has arms that move up and down, fingers must be placed so they can't be squeezed between the top arm or a knob that might be on the top blade clamp and the surface of the workpiece. This caution becomes more important as the thickness of the work increases. It's also important not to reach under the table while the tool is running.

*Fig. 3-1.* On a fixed-arm machine, only the plunger and blade move up and down. The operator's concern is mainly to keep fingers away from the blade area.

*Fig. 3-2.* On C-arm and parallel-arm tools, arms move up and down together with the blade. Hands and fingers can be hurt if you place them between the surface of the work and the tool's upper arm. The thicker the stock, the greater the possibility that this might happen.

## USING HOLD-DOWNS

Always use the hold-downs and whatever guards that are on the tool (Figs. 3-3 and 3-4). You will notice that in many illustrations I apparently choose to ignore the rule. Not really: *If safety components are removed it's only so they won't hide what the photo is demonstrating.*

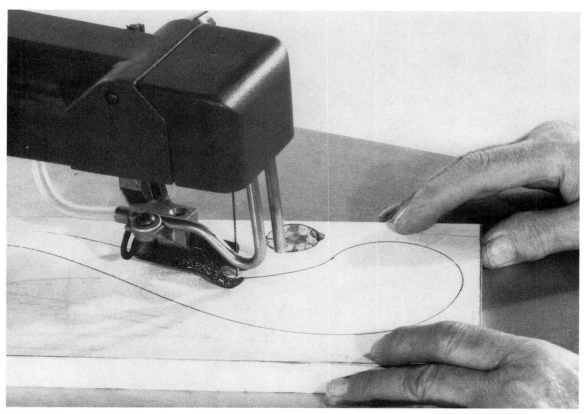

*Fig. 3-3.* Keep hold-downs and guards in place. The tubular guard on this Shopsmith tool also directs air to move sawdust from the cut line.

*Fig. 3-4.* The guard on the Craftsman machine serves well as a hold-down since it can be secured at various altitudes. Secure its lock knob as the guard rests lightly on the work.

The duty of a hold-down is to prevent the blade from lifting the work on its up stroke. The hold-down might be a spring affair, a plastic unit that also serves as a guard, or simply a shaped piece of steel like the one on some Hegner saws (Fig. 3-5), but, whatever, it should be placed so it barely touches the work. If the hold-down bears too heavily, it will interfere with moving the work and can even mar the work's surface. Don't depend entirely on a hold-down. It often happens, especially when making tight turns, that the blade might snag enough to cause the work to chatter

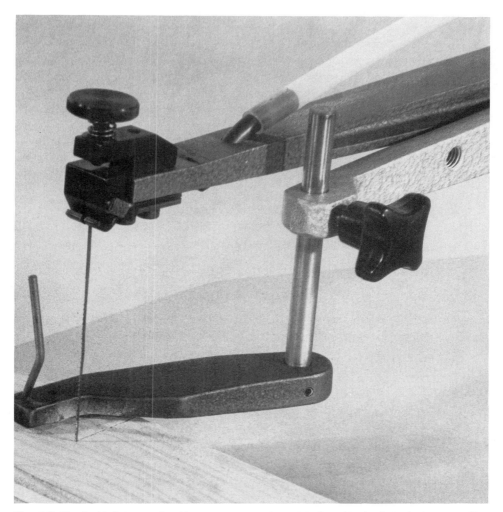

*Fig. 3-5.* The hold-down on the Hegner saw can be rotated and locked at whatever position you choose. The bent, vertical rod is the guard.

despite the hold-down, and it's those times that it is possible to get fingers pinched between the workpiece and the table. The answer is to always maintain sufficient pressure down on the work as you move it against the blade. Slow up work feed anytime you sense that the blade might snag.

## HAND POSITIONS

Be especially careful about how you use your fingers when sawing very small pieces. When possible, saw out small components from material that is large enough to keep your fingers away from the blade. Be aware that blades can break. Usually, the two pieces will continue to move on the same plane, but they might bend and point a jagged edge at a point away from the cut line. Machines that work with removable blade clamps provide for retaining the clamps should a blade break. Check the owner's manual and follow pertinent instructions.

Always release tension before removing a blade. It's good practice to be sure a blade has been installed correctly by manually causing it to move up and down before turning on the power. Always work with sharp blades and by applying only the amount of feed pressure that will keep the blade sawing easily and smoothly. Forcing the cut can only lead to premature blade breakage, bad work, and possible harm to you.

Work that is irregular in cross section, like molding, must be held very firmly so it won't rock while being sawed. Round materials, such as dowels and tubing, will tend to roll while being cut so secure them in a type of V-block that will be demonstrated in chapter 10.

## ILLUMINATION

Always provide sufficient illumination for the work area in general and for the tool in particular. Many manufacturers offer special lamps that can be mounted directly on the tool (Fig. 3-6). A tripod stand with an adjustable reflector makes a good substitute. Adjust lights so that shadows will not interfere with a clear view of the cut line.

## USING A FOOT SWITCH

A foot switch, like the one offered as an accessory for Hegner tools (Fig. 3-7), is a good addition because you can immediately turn off the machine without having to remove your hands from the workpiece while reaching for a switch. It is also a convenience if the blade has snagged and is causing the work to chatter. You can quickly shut down operations without losing control of the workpiece.

## PROTECT EYES, EARS, AND LUNGS

It doesn't take much coaxing to convince a woodworker of the importance of wearing safety goggles or a face mask to protect vision, but it seems more of a chore to

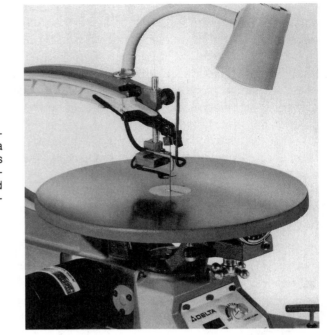

*Fig. 3-6.* Providing ample illumination on the tool's table is a safety factor. Accessory lamps are available for some machines. If not, consider a tripod stand with an adjustable reflector.

*Fig. 3-7.* A foot switch quickly turns the machine on or off. It's convenient for routine working because it frees hands for controlling the workpiece, and it allows quick shut-down of the tool should something untoward occur.

make the point that ears and lungs are also vulnerable to damage. Headphone-type hearing protectors are as important as any safety device. High frequencies can be generated by high-speed electric motors and by air movements that are generated by sawing procedures. A single exposure doesn't mean much, but effects, during frequent and prolonged usage of a machine, are cumulative and contribute to potential hearing damage. Acceptable hearing protectors provide a curtain against damaging high frequencies but will not shut out the normal woodworking noises or conversation you should hear.

The scroll saw doesn't spew out sawdust and other waste materials like some other shop machines, but, whether the residue is wood dust, metal, or plastic particles, it's best to avoid the possibility that you might breathe it in. So, wearing a dust mask is something you do for your own well being. If the mask is used with filters, as most are, be sure to replace the filter as often as necessary.

## DRESS FOR THE JOB

It's not unusual to find people who are not aware of the importance of having a special uniform for shop work. Heavy, nonslip shoes, preferably with steel toes, and tight-fitting shirts and trousers are sensible choices. I don't believe in wearing gloves. A necktie or any loose-fitting clothing that might catch on a tool—whether it is running or idle—is a no-no. Jewelry—rings, wristwatches, bracelets, and similar items— are adornments for social events; inside the shop they are hazards no matter what tool you are working with. Providing a cover for your hair, no matter if it is long or short, is important for protection from dust as well as for safety.

## SHOP ENVIRONMENT

Treat your shop as if it were a gourmet chef's kitchen. Maintain tables, benches, tool surfaces, and the floor in pristine condition. You definitely have a vacuum cleaner for the house, why not a shop-type for the woodworking area? The units are available in various sizes and price ranges, and most will have an exhaust port so the unit also can be used as a blower. Frequently remove the dirt and gummy substances that can accumulate on tool tables.

Cleaning solvents, used carefully by following the directions on the container, are often sufficient to return the table to proper condition. In extreme cases, you can work over the table with a pad sander that is fitted with a very fine emery abrasive. The weight of the sander is enough to supply necessary pressure, so forcing isn't necessary as you keep the sander moving. Wipe the table with a lint-free cloth and then apply a generous coating of paste wax. Rub the wax to a fine polish after it is dry. Repeat the waxing procedure frequently to protect the table and so that workpieces will move smoothly and easily during sawing procedures.

## SHOP BEHAVIOR

Overreaching, no matter what the operation or the tool, is bad practice, because you can get off balance or move your body to where it should not be. Don't try to be self-reliant when it is necessary to saw oversize workpieces, such as panel materials. Have someone supply extra support, after explaining the procedure, or use an outboard support, such as a roller-top stand.

Don't work with dull cutters. Sawed edges will not be acceptable, and having to exert extra feed pressure to keep the work moving will pose the possibility that your hands might slip.

Have the tool plugged in only when you are sawing. If you are cleaning the machine, or doing alignment checks, or mounting a saw blade, and so on, take the precaution of removing the plug from the power source. Check to be sure the switch is in the off position before you plug in. It's not advisable to leave the tool running while you attend to another chore, regardless of how little time is involved. Always wait for the cutting tool to stop before you move away from the machine.

The workshop is not a place for socializing. Don't try to work and visit at the same time. Let friends and neighbors know that they should not barge into your shop if they hear a tool running. You don't want to be startled.

The primary rule is always be alert. What you are doing should occupy all your attention. Don't do shopwork if you are tired, or upset, or after taking medicine or an alcoholic drink. Under such conditions it will be better to read a book or even to watch television.

## TOOL PRACTICE

Keep the machine in pristine condition and be sure to follow the manufacturer's instructions if lubrication is necessary. It's usually wise to use only those commercial accessories that are made for the tool you own. If the tool makes strange noises or doesn't operate as it should, check the owner's manual for a possible solution. If you don't find one, it's best to contact the supplier to find what the next step should be.

Always securely bolt the scroll saw to its own stand or to a solid workbench. If, despite this, the tool tends to move when used, or there is excessive vibration, secure the stand to the shop floor.

Prevent unauthorized use by removing the tool's switch key, if it has one, and hiding it. If this can't be done, then keep the shop locked, with the key in your own secret place. It's always possible to install a lockable master switch on an electrical entry box that feeds the shop tools.

## ELECTRICAL CONSIDERATIONS

Scroll saws are not double insulated as many portable tools are, so they are supplied with a 3-conductor cord and a grounding type plug that should be used in a matching 3-conductor grounded-type outlet as shown in Fig. 3-8. If the outlet available for

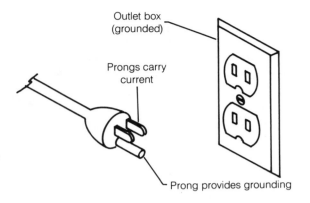

Outlet box
(grounded)

Prongs carry
current

Prong provides grounding

*Fig. 3-8.* Scroll saws are supplied with a 3-conductor cord and a grounded-type plug. It's dangerous to remove or alter the grounding prong in any way.

the machine is of the 2-prong type, an adapter can be used between the plug and the outlet (Fig. 3-9). Never remove or alter the grounding prong in any way. There are several important factors to be aware of regarding adapters. Consider them a temporary solution and only use them if you are sure that the 2-prong receptacle is correctly grounded. If there is doubt about the security of the system, have it checked by a qualified electrician. The use of the adapter is not permitted in Canada.

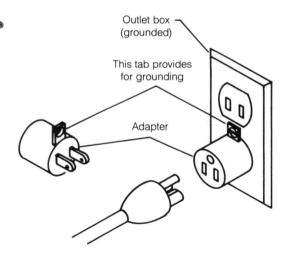

Outlet box
(grounded)

This tab provides
for grounding

Adapter

*Fig. 3-9.* An adapter can be used if the available receptacle is a 2-hole type—but you must be certain that the outlet is properly grounded. If in doubt, have the system checked by an electrician.

Be sure to check the owner's manual for other information regarding the electrical system the tool should be connected to—sizes and types of fuses or circuit breakers, types and sizes of extension cords should you ever use the tool away from the shop, and so on. Do not use the machine in damp or wet environments.

# Chapter 4

# The Basics of Scroll Sawing

**T**HE SCROLL SAW IS A MACHINE WHOSE PRIMARY FUNCTION IS TO SAW WOOD AND SOME nonwood materials. That's its job—to work with a variety of saw blades, to saw. The extent to which the tool can be useful in a shop relates directly to the user's interest in exploiting the function to its extreme. This involves starting with essentials, such as proper machine setup and learning basic work handling. This is the foundation on which to build toward the expertise that is available to anyone.

## SETTING UP

A scroll saw works best when it is established to minimize, if not eliminate, vibration. Most units will shake to some extent if they are simply set down on a surface; some to the point where they will meander voluntarily. A simple solution is to bolt the tool to an existing piece of shop furniture, like a sturdy workbench, but this cuts down on space that should be available for other chores, such as assembling projects. It's better to view the tool as an independent unit on its own stand.

The stand can be a metal one, offered by the manufacturer—usually as an accessory—or a homemade wooden one. Commercial stands are open so they occupy cubic space that can be utilized for storage. A custom stand can be designed to solve the problem. The basic structure of a stand that is sturdy and not difficult to make is shown in Fig. 4-1. It can be assembled as shown so you can get to mounting a tool pretty quickly, and then completed in your own good time by adding a back, hinged door, and interior shelves.

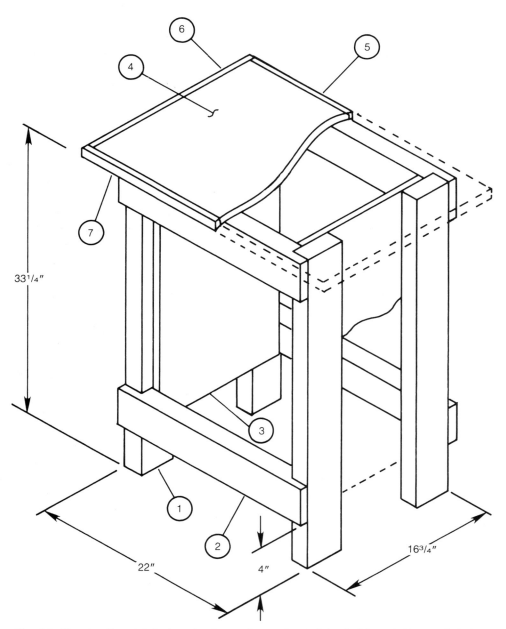

*Fig. 4-1.* Construction details for a basic scroll-saw stand. A back, hinged door, and shelves can be added.

Materials list for machine stand (Fig. 4-1)

| Key | Part | PCS | Size | Material |
|-----|------|-----|------|----------|
| 1 | legs | 4 | $1^1/_2 \times 3^1/_2 \times 33^1/_4$ | fir |
| 2 | rails | 4 | $1^1/_2 \times 3^1/_2 \times 22$ | " |
| 3 | sides | 2 | $^3/_4 \times 15^1/_4 \times 29^1/_4$ | plywood |
| 4 | top | 1 | $^3/_4 \times 18^1/_2 \times 26^1/_2$ | " |
| 5 | trim | 1 | $^3/_4 \times ^3/_4 \times 26^1/_2$ | fir |
| 6 | trim | 2 | $^3/_4 \times ^3/_4 \times 19^1/_4$ | " |
| 7 | trim | 1 | $^3/_4 \times ^3/_4 \times 28$ | " |

(Dim. in inches)

A question with scroll sawing is whether it is better to sit or stand. It's really a moot point. An operator doesn't have to be advised that it might be less tiring to sit during extended operations, or that it's not necessary to sit when a cut requires but a few seconds.

A way to go is to keep a draftsman's stool handy; one that is adjustable in height so the operator can be comfortable while having a clear view of the work area (Fig. 4-2). A solution that doesn't require a separate piece of furniture is to hinge a seat to the machine so it is always ready to use but out of the way when not needed (Figs. 4-3 and 4-4). The idea is practical but should be incorporated only if the machine is bolted to the floor. If not, the weight of even a small person can cause the machine to tip forward. The construction details shown in Fig. 4-5 worked out nicely for the stand that is available for the new Delta scroll saw. Some modifications probably will be needed to adapt the design to other units.

The idea that is shown in Fig. 4-6 can be used pretty much as is for any scroll saw that is mounted on its own stand. It's like having the machine bolted to a movable floor. The skid is long enough to provide ample standing room for the operator whose own weight provides additional stability for the tool. The project can be enhanced a bit by adding a seat that can be moved to and fro, or removed when not in use (Fig. 4-7). The seat height is not adjustable, but if you wish to change its height from what is suggested in the drawing (Fig. 4-8), you need only shorten or lengthen the two sides.

## WORK SUPPORT

For most scroll-saw work the table that is part of the machine will provide adequate support, but there might be times, especially when doing saber sawing on panels, when outboard support is needed to keep the work on the correct plane. Good support also is a safety factor because you can concentrate on sawing without having to strain to keep the work in position. Roller-top stands that can be adjusted for height are available commercially, or you can custom make one like the unit shown in Fig. 4-9.

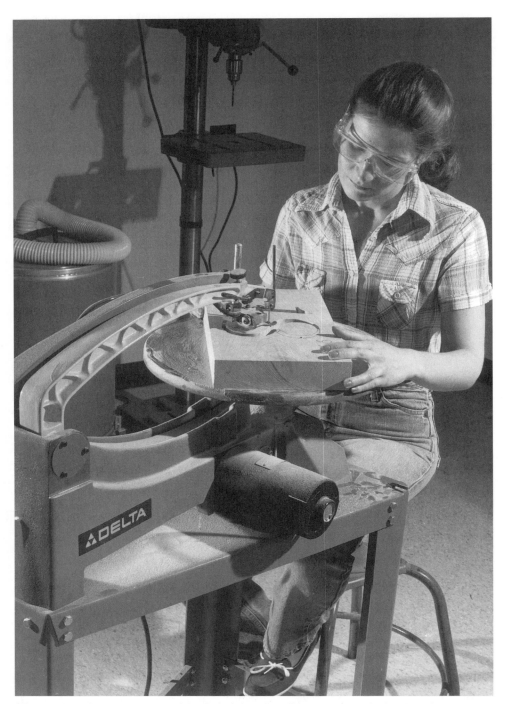

*Fig. 4-2.* A draftsmans-type stool that is height-adjustable can serve nicely when the operator decides to sit during extended sawing procedures.

*Fig. 4-3.* A hinged support that eliminates the need for additional shop furniture can serve as a seat.

*Fig. 4-4.* The seat pivots out of the way when it is not needed. Do not copy this design unless the machine is bolted to the floor.

The roller used on the prototype is a metal tube that is sealed at each end with wooden discs that are sized for a tight fit (Fig. 4-10), but you can substitute a large round of wood, something in the nature of a closet pole. The axles for the roller are 1/4-inch bolts that turn in oversize holes drilled through the metal support brackets.

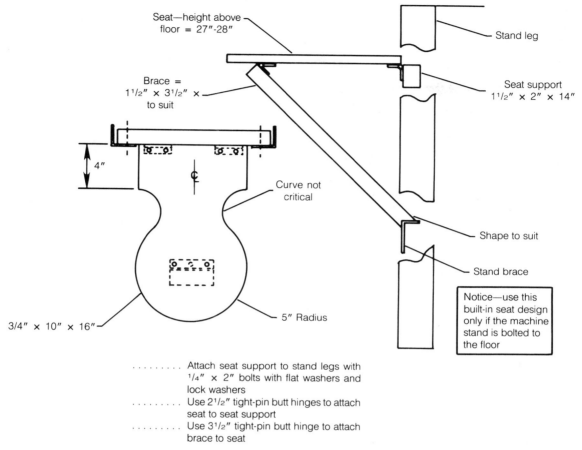

Seat—height above
floor = 27"-28"

Stand leg

Brace =
1¹/₂" × 3¹/₂" ×
to suit

Seat support
1¹/₂" × 2" × 14"

4"

Curve not
critical

Shape to suit

Stand brace

3/4" × 10" × 16"

5" Radius

Notice—use this
built-in seat design
only if the machine
stand is bolted to
the floor

. . . . . . . . . Attach seat support to stand legs with
¹/₄" × 2" bolts with flat washers and
lock washers
. . . . . . . . . Use 2¹/₂" tight-pin butt hinges to attach
seat to seat support
. . . . . . . . . Use 3¹/₂" tight-pin butt hinge to attach
brace to seat

*Fig. 4-5.* Construction details of the hinged seat. It might be necessary to change dimensions to suit a machine other than the new Delta scroll saw.

Because the homemade stand's height is adjustable, it is an all-purpose accessory that can supply additional work-support when using other machines; for example, band saws and table saws. Figure 4-11 provides the construction details for the stand.

## ALIGNMENT

The basic setting on a scroll saw calls for a 90-degree angle between the surface of the table and the saw blade. It's not wise simply to trust the zero setting on the table's tilt scale because they are seldom as accurate as you would like them to be. It's better to establish the correct setting by using a reliable square. There can be a problem though; because the length of blade that you can check against is relatively short, the square you own might be too large for the job. I believe that a specially made

*Fig. 4-6.* Mounting the tool on a skid is a way to provide stability. Situated so, the machine can still be moved about or placed in a storage area.

gauge that will always be available is a better way to go. The gauge isn't more than a length of hardwood that has been carefully sawed and sanded so all corners are perfectly square (Fig. 4-12).

Another check system is to first form a very shallow kerf in a length of wood that is as wide as the saw allows. Then, after rotating the wood 180 degrees, position it behind the blade to see if the blade aligns exactly with the kerf (Fig. 4-13). If it does, then the angle between blade and table is correct. If not, some slight adjustment of the table will be needed. When alignment is correct, secure the table's position and set the pointer on the tilt scale exactly on the zero mark. Go through the checking procedure periodically. It's also a good idea to occasionally check sawed edges with a square.

## BLADE CONSIDERATIONS

How a blade is mounted in its clamps and installed in the machine depends entirely on the design of the scroll saw. Some, especially those that work with pin-type blades, require that the blade be mounted directly between upper and lower arms. Others, concepts that are becoming more prevalent, permit the mounting of blades in clamps that are removed from the machine (Figs. 4-14 and 4-15). The latter idea, especially on C-arm and parallel-arm designs, ensures that blades will be correctly

Fig. 4-7. A removable seat that can be moved to and fro to suit the operator makes the skid idea even more practical.

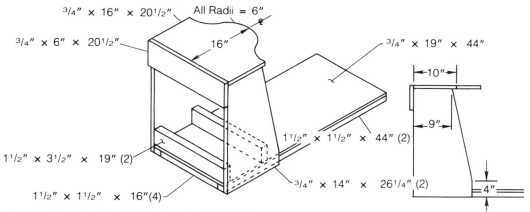

Fig. 4-8. How to make the skid/seat project. The height of the seat can be adjusted for individual preference simply by using a different length for the two sides.

*Fig. 4-9.* A roller-top, movable stand, can be placed anywhere about the machine to provide outboard support for extra large workpieces.

established before they are put to work. Because extra blade clamps are supplied or available as accessories, an assortment of blades can be on hand, ready to install, to suit the needs of several sawing requirements (Fig. 4-16).

Off-machine blade-mounting arrangements, as long as the user follows the instructions in the owner's manual, pretty much guarantee the correct vertical movement of the blade. On a fixed-arm machine, where blade chucks must allow for various blade widths, some attention is required to ensure that blades travel the path they should. Typical do's and don'ts are illustrated in Fig. 4-17.

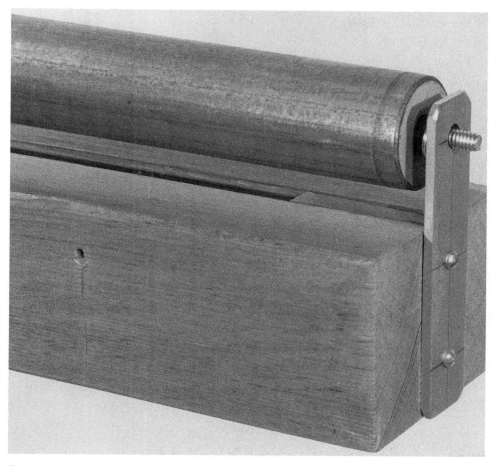

*Fig. 4-10.* A metal tube serves as the roller top for the support stand. The ends of the tube are sealed with tight-fitting wooden discs. Bolt/axles must be installed before the discs are forced into place.

## BLADE TENSION

There are machines, both constant-tension and fixed-arm designs, that have graduations or click-stop indications that suggest how the blade should be tensioned, but they offer only a place to start. The tension that is best for the blade and the operation lies in the operator's judgment and is best established by experimentally sawing in the project material. There must, however, be a place to start. One way, as good as any other after following the instructions in the owner's manual, is to adjust tensioning one way or the other while flicking the blade with a fingernail as if it were a guitar string. A nice-sounding "twang" can be accepted as a reasonable condition for sawing, at least to start with. Some experienced operators will make this test while

Materials list—outboard support stand (Fig. 4-1)

| Key | Part | PCS | Size | Material |
|---|---|---|---|---|
| 1 | post | 1 | $1\frac{1}{2} \times 2 \times 30$ | hardwood |
| 2 | case | 2 | $\frac{3}{4} \times 3\frac{1}{2} \times 30$ | plywood |
| 3 | case | 2 | $\frac{3}{4} \times 1\frac{1}{2} \times 30$ | " |
| 4 | feet | 4 | $\frac{3}{4} \times 6 \times 11$ | " |
| 5 | roller support | 2 | $1\frac{1}{2} \times 2\frac{1}{2} \times 18\frac{1}{2}$ | hardwood |
| 6 | filler | 2 | $\frac{1}{2} \times 2 \times 2\frac{1}{2}$ | " |
| 7 | holder | 2 | $\frac{1}{8} \times 1 \times 4\frac{1}{4}$ | aluminum |
| 8 | roller | 1 | $1\frac{1}{2}$ OD $\times 18$ | rigid rubing |
| 9 | plug | 2 | $1\frac{1}{2} \times 1\frac{1}{2} \times 1\frac{1}{2}$ | hardwood |

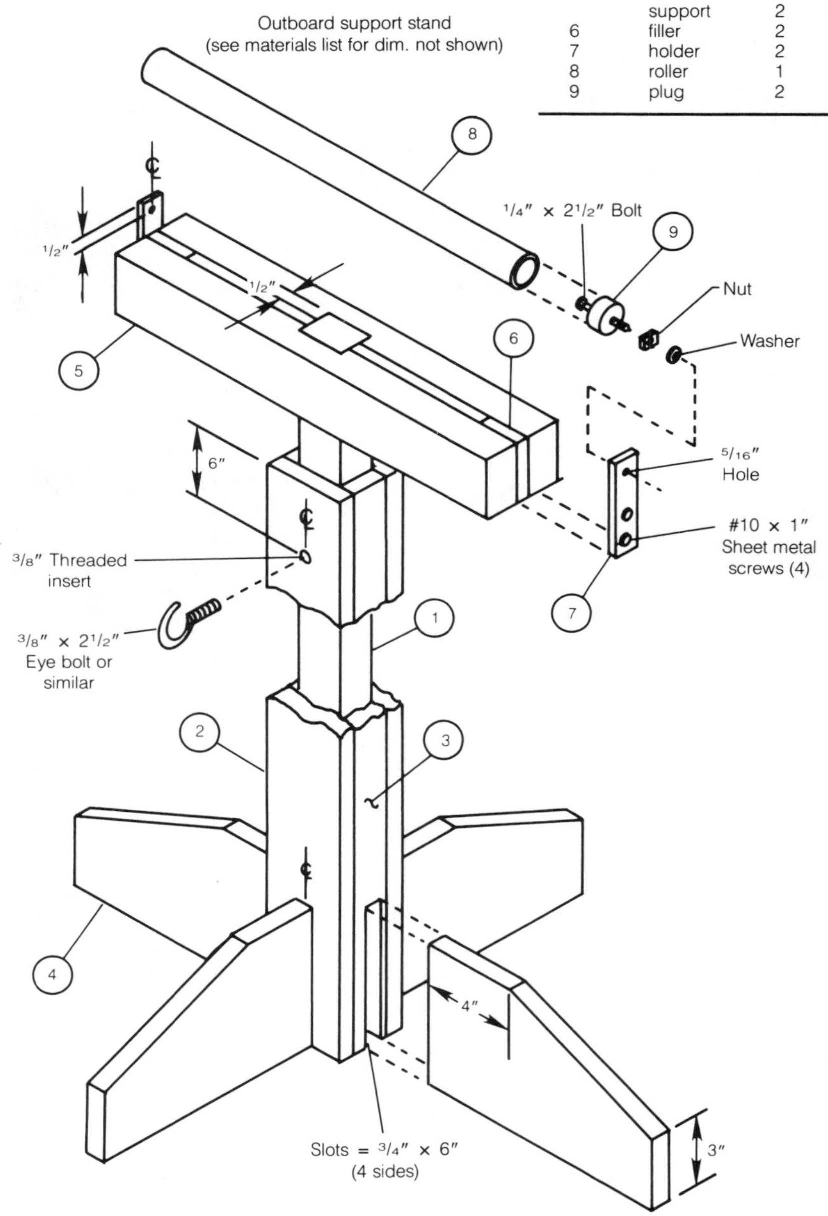

Outboard support stand
(see materials list for dim. not shown)
8
1/4" × 2 1/2" Bolt
9
Nut
Washer
1/2"
1/2"
5
6
6"
5/16"
Hole
#10 × 1"
Sheet metal
screws (4)
3/8" Threaded
insert
7
1
3/8" × 2 1/2"
Eye bolt or
similar
2
3
4
4"
3"
Slots = 3/4" × 6"
(4 sides)


*Fig. 4-11.* How to make the roller-top, outboard support stand.

*Fig. 4-12.* A gauge for checking the basic angle between blade and table can be a length of hardwood that has been sawed and sanded so that all corners are perfectly square.

the machine is running, but that is a procedure I do not recommend. It is logical that, generally, a slim blade should have more tension than a wide, coarse blade. Overall, how cutting gets along, the results obtained, whether blades last an acceptable period of time, compose the criteria of good blade tension. One of the sawing results that indicates attention is needed is blade "drift" (Fig. 4-18). This kind of result on sawed edges is more likely with slim blades than with heavy, coarse blades.

*Fig. 4-13.* Saw a shallow kerf in a length of wood and then place it behind the blade after rotating it 180 degrees. You will know that the blade is square to the table if blade and kerf mate correctly.

## ILLUMINATION

Adequate illumination directed to the area where the blade should be following the pattern line is important for accuracy. An accessory lamp that can be attached to the top arm of the machine, or a separate stand with adjustable reflector can be included in the machine setup. It's not unusual to find that some operators, when involved with

*Fig. 4-14.* Being able to mount blades correctly before they are installed in the machine is a nice convenience. The table on the Sears/Craftsman tool has cast pockets that hold the blade clamps while the blade is secured.

highly detailed operations that involve precise sawing, will work with a magnifying glass. Some manufacturers—Hegner is one—offer as an accessory a magnifier with a built-in light that can be attached directly to the machine. An alternative is to provide a large, conventional magnifying glass by mounting it on the upper arm-cover of the machine in a manner suggested in Fig. 4-19.

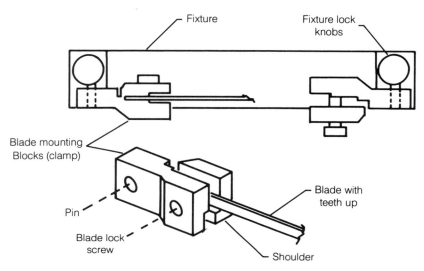

*Fig. 4-15.* Methods used for off-machine mounting of blades can differ. This fixture, that is supplied with the tool, is Shopsmith's way of doing it. In all cases, obey the instructions that are in the owners manual.

*Fig. 4-16.* Extra blade clamps, if not supplied with the machine, are available as accessories. Having several sets is a way to keep an assortment of blades ready for quick mounting in the tool.

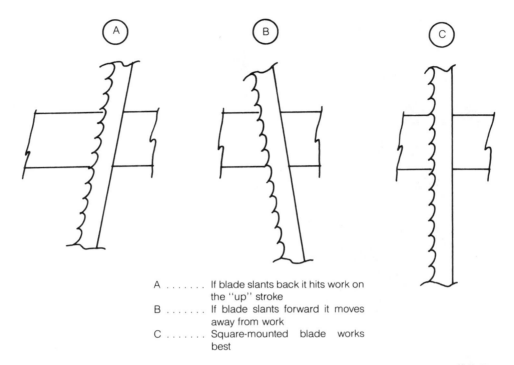

A ....... If blade slants back it hits work on the "up" stroke
B ....... If blade slants forward it moves away from work
C ....... Square-mounted blade works best

*Fig. 4-17.* On fixed-arm machines, you must be careful to install the blade so it will move on a true vertical line. Some operators prefer a slight cant forward at the top end. Justification is that the action will help to clear sawdust from the kerf. It's not a good idea, though, if the pattern requires pivot-turns.

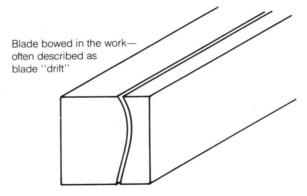

Blade bowed in the work—
often described as
blade "drift"

*Fig. 4-18.* Blade "drift" is an indication that you are using the wrong blade for the job or that blade-tension needs an adjustment.

The mounting bracket for the sample is a length of $1/8$-inch × 1-inch aluminum, bent appropriately, and drilled at one end for the hole in the handle of the glass and at the opposite end for the bolt normally used for a lamp attachment. Actually, both a lamp and the glass can be mounted together. Adjust the glass, with the power off, to

*Fig. 4-19.* You can install an ordinary magnifying glass by following the suggestions in the text. Seeing through the glass takes a little getting used to, so start carefully.

be sure it can't be hit by an oscillating arm or, if mounted on a fixed-arm tool, by plunger and blade. Looking through the glass takes some getting used to, so work carefully.

## MINIMIZE FEATHERING/SPLINTERING

There will be some feathering or splintering on the bottom of workpieces, the degree depending on the density of the material and the size of the blade. A solution, on work that requires extra care, and when the tool's table has an insert, is to supply a special insert that is drilled so the blade in use will have zero clearance (Fig. 4-20). The insert, which can be metal or a dense hardboard, should fit tightly in the table opening.

Another method, usable on any machine, is demonstrated in Fig. 4-21. A piece of plywood or hardboard is carefully kerfed and then secured to the table with clamps or with double-face tape if clamps hinder moving the work. Whatever the method, it must support the work as close to the blade as possible.

## FEED-SWING

An important consideration for good work handling is demonstrated by the simple example in Fig. 4-22. Assuming a 1/2-inch-radius cut in material that is X inches square, you can see that the radius of the feed-swing must be much greater than that of the cut to keep the blade on the pattern line. This factor, to a degree that is affected by the pattern and work size, applies to all scroll sawing that involves curves.

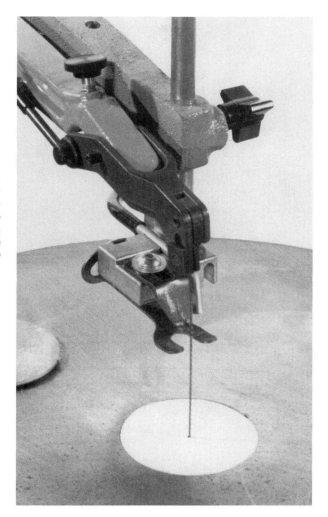

*Fig. 4-20.* A substitute, home-made insert that allows no clearance around the blade is one way to minimize the feathering that can occur when the blade leaves the bottom surface of the workpiece.

## QUICK TURNS

It's often necessary to abruptly change the direction of work-feed to stay on a pattern line. The technique, which is most successful with fine blades and spiral blades, is to quickly rotate the workpiece using the blade as a pivot point. The amount of rotation required depends on the pattern but it can be anything, even a full circle so the blade, when necessary, can actually return in its own kerf without having to move off line to do so (Figs. 4-23 and 4-24).

Doing pivot, or spot turns, successfully takes some practice. Successfully means that the radius of the turn won't be more than the blade's width. The narrower the blade, the tighter the turn can be. It's obvious that the pivot turning can't be accomplished with wide blades. Don't be too cautious when practicing. It's more

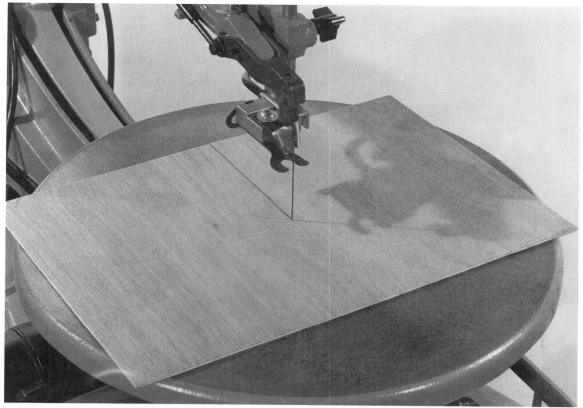

*Fig. 4-21.* This is another way to provide for zero clearance around the blade. Use double-face tape or clamps to keep the auxiliary platform in place.

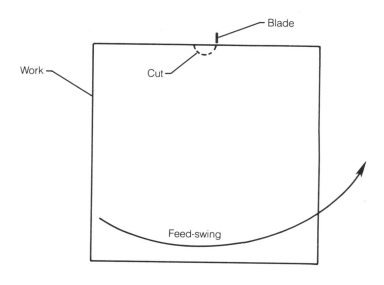

Blade

Work

Cut

Feed-swing

*Fig. 4-22.* This is an example of "feed-swing." The radius of the arc in which you move the work must be much greater than the radius of the cut.

*Fig. 4-23.* A good pivot turn (arrow) will not be obvious. Here, the work has been rotated 180 degrees so the blade can retreat through its own kerf.

likely that the blade will move off line if you try to make the turn very slowly. Learn how to keep the work secure as you quickly rotate it.

The advantage of pivot turning is demonstrated in Fig. 4-25 where the procedure allows the cut to be made in one continuous pass. Other methods for sawing the same pattern without pivot turning, but nevertheless perfectly acceptable fashion, are shown in Figs. 4-26 and 4-27.

## VARIOUS SAWING METHODS

Points that are on the perimeter of a pattern can be sawed in one pass if pivot turns are used at any corners that are involved (Fig. 4-28). Other methods are necessary when, for example, the width of the blade won't allow a sharp turn. In one, (Fig. 4-29) a loop return is made to the point and the cut is continued to where it leaves the

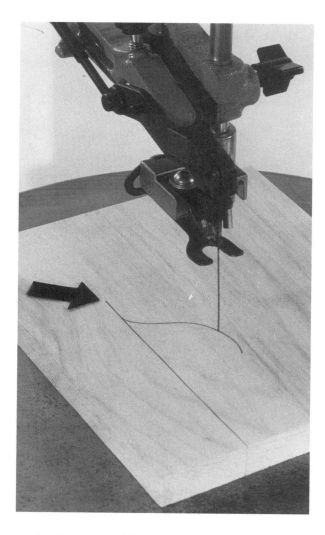

*Fig. 4-24.* Pivot-turning and re-treating from the point allows, among other things, leaving a clean line while you get to another area of the pattern. Arrow indicates where the pivot-turn was made.

work. Then, two additional short cuts are needed to remove the waste that remains. A second method is similar but calls for the backtracking that is shown in Fig. 4-30. In this case, a single additional cut will finish the job.

Sharp inside or outside corners can be handled as shown in Fig. 4-31 when the blade in use can't make an abrupt turn. For the inside corner, backtrack only to the point where the blade can easily leave the original kerf to travel the loop back to the corner. The outside corner can, of course, be accomplished with two passes. The loop method, when the pattern or the part that is needed allows its use, avoids the backtracking that is required by the two-pass system.

Inside, rectangular, and similar shapes that have sharp corners require the backtracking that is shown in the example in Fig. 4-32. Retreat out of the first cut and

*Fig. 4-25.* Using the pivot-turn technique made it possible to follow the pattern line accurately in a continuous pass.

make the second cut to the corner. Backtrack only to the point where you can loop to the first corner. A final short cut will finish the job.

## CIRCULAR SAWING

A good way to learn how a blade behaves in relation to wood grain direction is to do some practicing by sawing circles. You will find that sawing and following a pattern line is easier when going across the grain of the wood. When sawing with the grain, the blade cuts more slowly and it will have a tendency to follow wood grain rather than a marked line.

Because cross-grain cutting is a littler easier to do, it's a good idea when sawing circles or arcs to start the cut at a cross-grain point. Working with a piece of wood with dimensions that equal the diameter of the circle is not the best way to go, because the blade will run out and will have to reenter at each end of perpendicular diameters (Fig. 4-33). It is better to work with stock that is a bit larger than necessary so that only one entry cut is needed and sawing can be completed in a single pass (Fig. 4-34). If you work so, the perimeter of the disc will be much smoother than it would be if you had to move on and off the pattern line four times. The same thought applies, as illustrated in Fig. 4-35, even when the project is not a full circle. A pivot-guide system like the one shown in Fig. 4-36 can be used to saw perfect circles. I will talk more about the idea and application techniques in chapter 10.

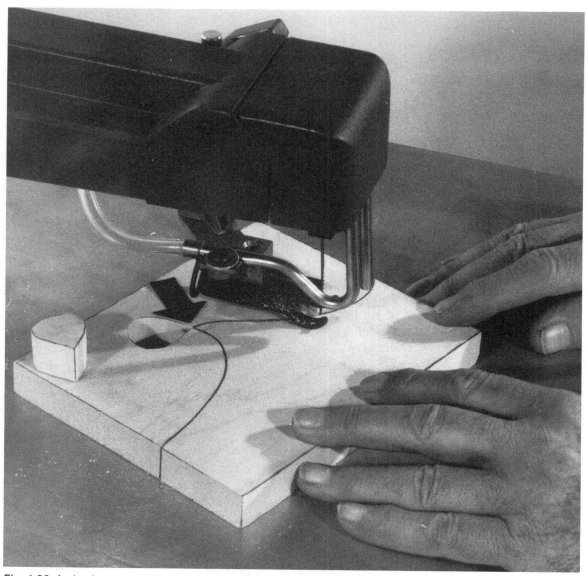

*Fig. 4-26.* A circular return at the point of the pattern also allows the cut to be made in a single pass. The size of the loop you must follow will depend on the thickness of the stock and the blade being used.

## STRAIGHT SAWING

Straight cuts, whether done across the grain (crosscutting) or parallel with the grain (ripping) are feasible on a scroll saw so long as you stay aware of some relevant factors (Figs. 4-37 and 4-38). For one thing, it's wise to avoid using very slim blades because they will have a greater tendency than wide ones to wander off line, espe-

*Fig. 4-27.* When a point of a pattern is on an edge of the stock, it can be accomplished in two passes. Here, the first cut has been made to the point (arrow) and the second cut is in progress.

cially when ripping. Many blades will tend to *lead*, that is, voluntarily veer slightly from a marked line. Some are more guilty of this than others, so, if you plan a lot of straight cutting, it will pay to try a few blades to see which one works best.

A common correction when freehandedly moving material and blade lead is evident, is to adjust the angle of feed to compensate. The adjustment is seldom more

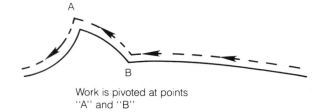

Work is pivoted at points
"A" and "B"

*Fig. 4-28.* Pivot-turning allows a pattern like this to be accomplished in a single pass.

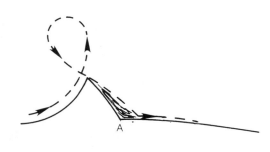

*Fig. 4-29.* One way to use the loop return when the blade must move to a sharp corner is to bypass the area. The remaining waste is removed with two additional cuts.

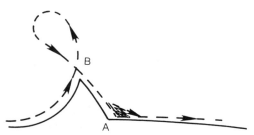

Make loop return to point "A"—backtrack to "B" and continue—final cut will remove remaining waste (shaded)

*Fig. 4-30.* Another method involves a bit of backtracking. In this case, just a single additional cut will remove remaining waste.

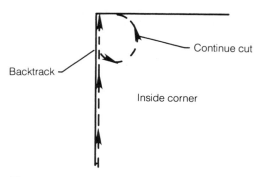
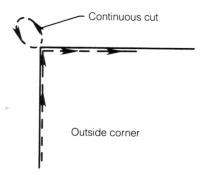

*Fig. 4-31.* Methods that can be used to form sharp inside or outside corners.

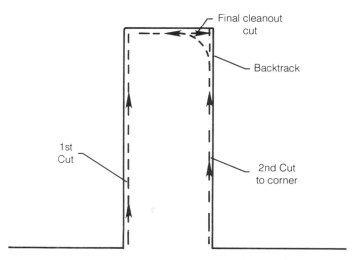

Fig. 4-32. Rectangular cutouts can be handled this way. If the shape were to have rounded corners instead of square, it would be wise to drill holes to supply the arcs. Three straight saw cuts would complete the job.

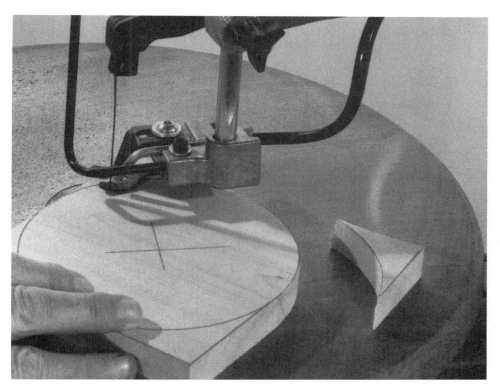

Fig. 4-33. Using material that is exactly right for the size of a disc is not a good way to go. The blade would run out at four points, each of which would require further attention for smoothness.

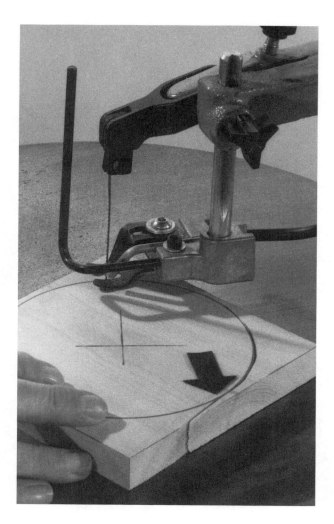

*Fig. 4-34.* It's better, when sawing circles, to use stock that is a bit larger than you need. Then, just one entry cut is needed (arrow), and the job can be finished with a continuous pass.

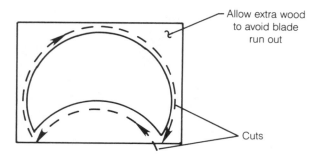

Allow extra wood to avoid blade run out

Cuts

*Fig. 4-35.* Forms like this always turn out better when continuous cuts are made possible by drawing the pattern on oversize stock.

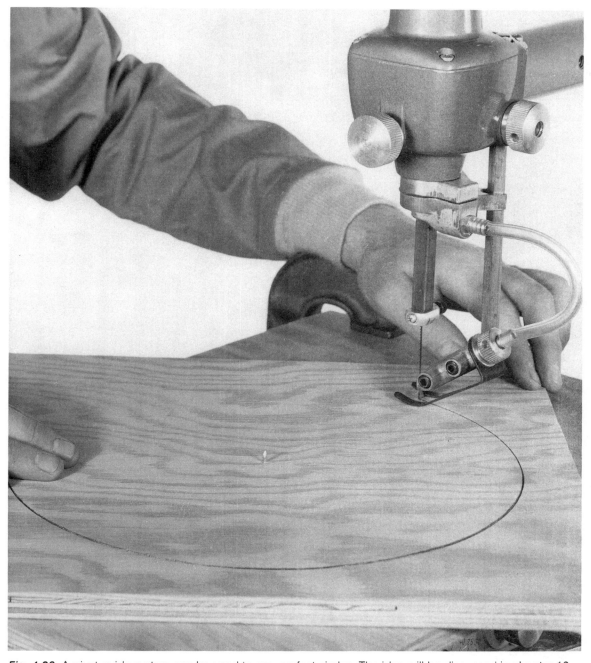

*Fig. 4-36.* A pivot-guide system can be used to saw perfect circles. The idea will be discussed in chapter 10.

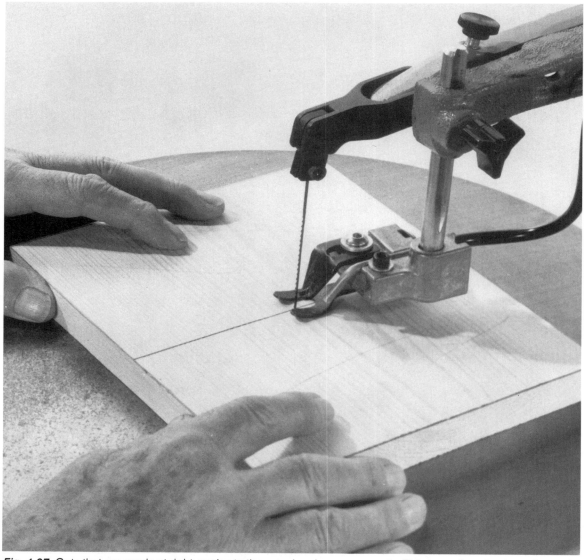

*Fig. 4-37.* Cuts that are made at right angles to the wood grain are *crosscuts*. This type of sawing is easier to do than cuts that are made WITH the grain.

than a few degrees. In all cases, a slower-than-usual feed speed will contribute to successful work (Fig. 4-39).

Although guided cuts are not the forte of scroll saws, it is not out of line to supply a guide for straight sawing, especially when many similar pieces are needed, so long as you are aware of possible blade faults. The design of the Sears/Craftsman machine goes along with the thought because its table is grooved for a miter gauge that is used as a guide for both crosscutting and ripping (Figs. 4-40 and 4-41).

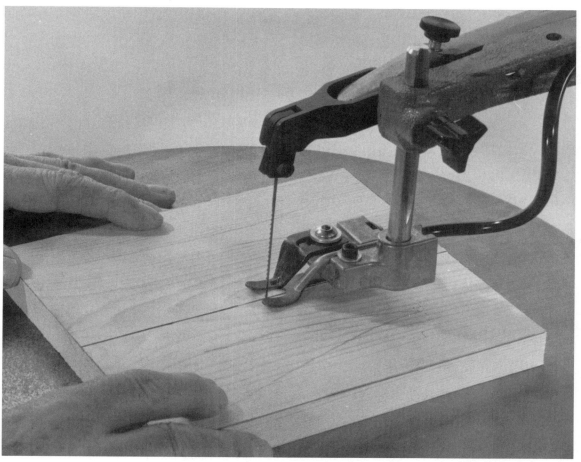

*Fig. 4-38.* Cuts that parallel the wood grain are *rip cuts*. More care is required than with crosscutting because the blade will have a tendency to follow grain lines instead of pattern lines.

For other machines, you can organize a T-shaped guide that can be clamped in place and used like a rip fence (Figs. 4-42 and 4-43). Actually, ideas of this nature should be utilized only when several pieces of equal width are needed. For a single component, you might as well do the job freehandedly.

Figure 4-44 demonstrates how a guide setup can be used to saw multiple, similar cutoffs. The workpiece is butted against the improvised fence for each cut and moved past the blade with a pusher that has a nail for a handle.

## FORMING SLOTS

The technique to use when forming slots will depend on whether the slot is open or closed and whether ends are round or square. When round ends are okay, the job will be easier to do if you first drill end holes with a diameter that equals the width of

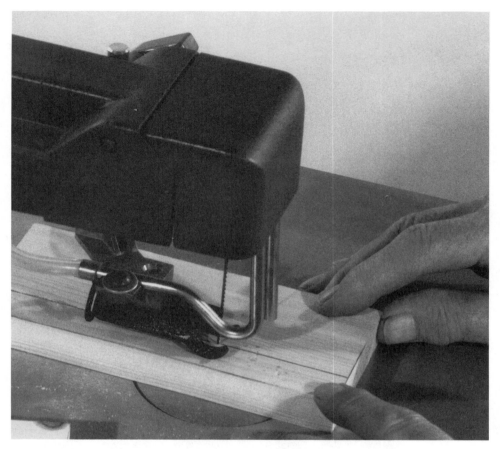

*Fig. 4-39.* Ripping can be done freehandedly with good results. If the blade tends to lead off the line, adjust the angle at which you move the work just a bit to compensate.

the slot. Straight cuts that can be done freehandedly or by working carefully with a guide fence will complete the job (Fig. 4-45). The same thought applies when slots must be contained within the borders of a workpiece (Fig. 4-46). The system to use for this and other types of internal cuts is *piercing*. The techniques for this scroll-saw exclusive will be discussed in chapter 5.

It's still okay to use starting holes if the slot must have square ends. This will allow easy removal of the bulk of the waste. Additional sawing will clean out the remaining corner arcs. The sawing procedure illustrated in Fig. 4-32 can be followed to form wide slots.

### BEVELS AND MITERS

Bevels are angular cuts that are made parallel with the direction of wood grain. When the cut removes the entire edge of the stock, the result is a *bevel*. The result is a

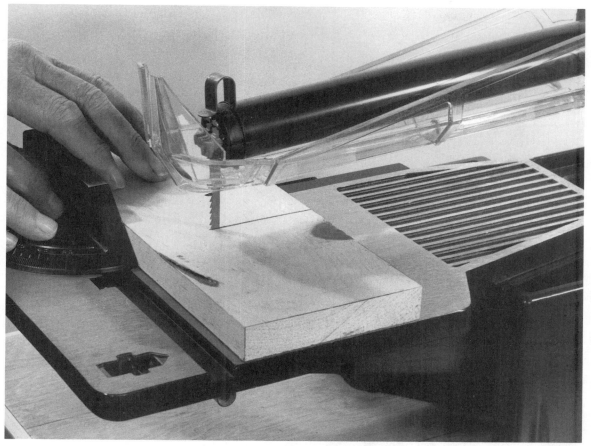

*Fig. 4-40.* The miter gauge that is provided with the Sears/Craftsman scroll saw is used to guide work for cross-cutting. Note the wide blade that is being used.

*chamfer* when only part of the edge—a top or bottom corner—is sawed off (Fig. 4-47).

Bevels are accomplished like rip cuts, except that the table is tilted to the angle that is required. When the work is done freehandedly, there is the additional chore of preventing the work from sliding away from the blade. Working with a guide, as demonstrated in Fig. 4-48, can make the job easier. As with all chores of this nature, good results will depend on how carefully you move the work and the use of a reasonably wide blade that is in prime condition.

The same setup can be used should you wish to chamfer top and bottom edges of the work or to create a point. Just make a second pass after the stock has been inverted and turned end-for-end (Figs. 4-49 and 4-50).

*Fig. 4-41.* The miter gauge, when locked in place so its head is parallel with the side of the blade, is used like a rip fence.

Miters are angular cuts that are made across the grain (Fig. 4-51). Cross-miters also are done across the grain but on an angle to the surface of the material (Fig. 4-52). Accuracy, when cuts like this are made for joints, is critical. Part of a degree of error doesn't seem like much, but when it is multiplied eight times as it would be, for example, in the case of a 4-sided frame, there would be much frustration at assembly time.

## PAD SAWING

Pad sawing is the technique to use when two or more duplicate components are required. The idea saves time and effort and ensures duplication (Figs. 4-53 and 4-54). Execution is simple—a matter of assembling individual pieces with the pattern

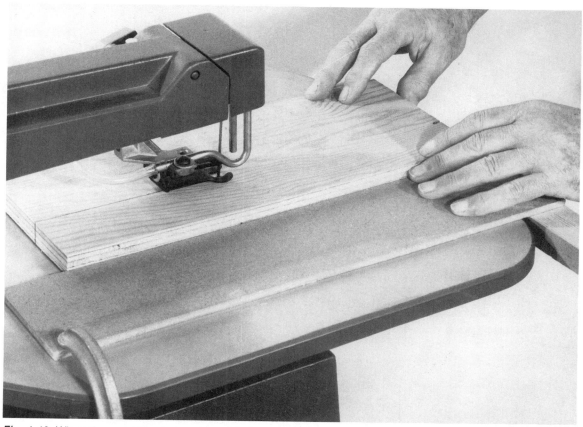

*Fig. 4-42.* When the machine does not provide for a fence, you can organize for guided ripping by making a T-shaped guide.

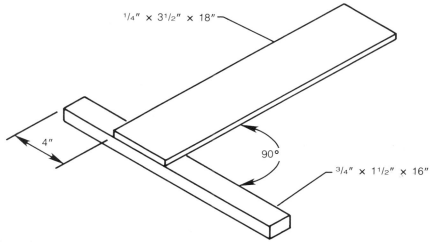

1/4″ × 3 1/2″ × 18″

4″

90°

3/4″ × 1 1/2″ × 16″

*Fig. 4-43.* A T-shaped guide for ripping can be used on any square or rectangular table.

*Fig. 4-44.* Cutting off similar pieces can be done accurately if you use a jig setup like this. Work is moved past the blade with a block that has a large nail as a handle.

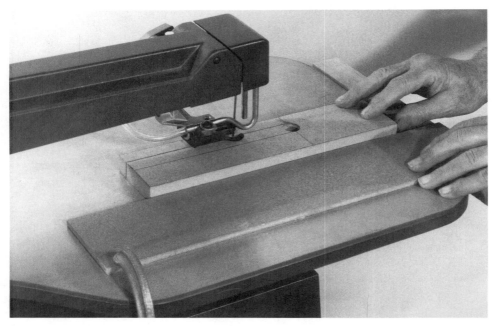

*Fig. 4-45.* Round-ends slots are easy to produce if you start by drilling an end hole whose diameter equals the width of the slot. Two straight cuts that you can do freehandedly or with a guide as shown here, finish the job.

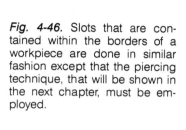

*Fig. 4-46.* Slots that are contained within the borders of a workpiece are done in similar fashion except that the piercing technique, that will be shown in the next chapter, must be employed.

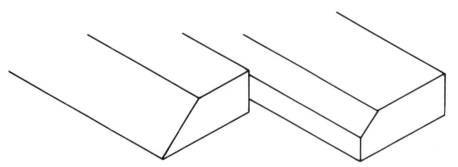

*Fig. 4-47.* The shape at the left is a *bevel*; that on the right is a *chamfer*.

marked on the top layer and then sawing as if the pad were a solid block of wood (Fig. 4-55).

Plies for the pad can be held together with nails that are driven into waste areas or by using double-face tape between layers. Use the tape in waste areas because the material is adhesive enough to lift surface fibers from the wood when it is removed. Masking tape, used as if you were wrapping a package, is another possibility, but be careful when placing it. Sawing might remove enough of the tape so that plies will not stay in the pad as they should.

The number of duplicates you can cut is limited by the depth of cut of the machine and, of course, by the thickness of the pieces (Fig. 4-56). If the machine has a 2-inch depth of cut, you can saw eight pieces of 1/4-inch-thick wood, but only four pieces if the material thickness is 1/2 inch.

*Fig. 4-48.* Beveling is done like ripping, the difference being that the tool's table is tilted to the angle that is required.

*Fig. 4-49.* Use the same technique to chamfer edges or to form a point on the edge of the stock by inverting it and turning it end-for-end and then making a second pass.

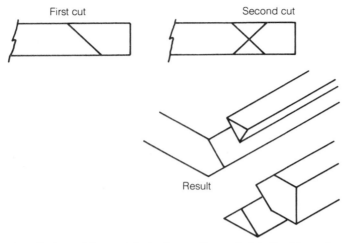

First cut

Second cut

Result

*Fig. 4-50.* The steps that result in a pointed edge on the material. The triangular waste pieces can serve as glue blocks.

*Fig. 4-51.* When an angular cut is made across the grain of the wood it is called a "miter." Be sure of accuracy when making this type of cut especially if it is needed as part of a joint.

*Fig. 4-52.* A cross-miter is a cut that angles from the work's surfaces. It can be accomplished on the Sears/Craftsman tool by tilting the blade. On other machines it is necessary to tilt the table.

*Fig. 4-53.* Pad sawing is the way to go when you need several duplicate pieces. The technique involves assembling layers of material so they can be sawed as if they were a solid block.

*Fig. 4-54.* These six brackets, made of 1/4-inch-thick plywood, were cut as a pad. Not much of a chore for most any scroll saw.

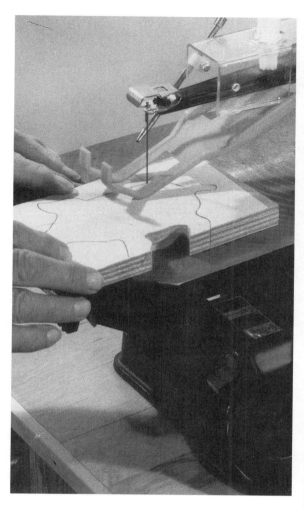

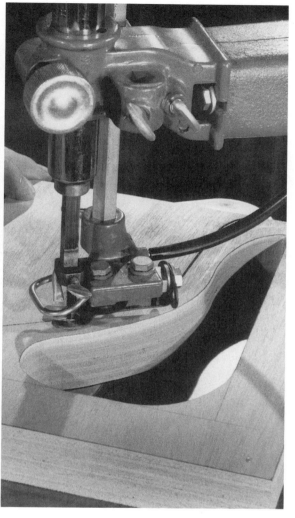

Fig. 4-55. The pattern is attached or drawn on the surface of the top layer of the pad. Sawing proceeds in normal fashion. Be sure the angle between the blade and the table is 90 degrees.

Fig. 4-56. Piercing also can be accomplished when the pad-sawing system is used.

Always check the angle between blade and table before doing pad sawing. If it isn't 90 degrees, pieces in the pad will have beveled edges and they will differ in size.

## TROUBLESHOOTING

When things go wrong, check the information that is offered in Fig. 4-57 for a possible solution. The chart covers operations, such as metal sawing, sanding and filing, that were not covered in this chapter, but I will be getting to them.

# Troubleshooting chart

| | The problem | Possible causes | What to check for or do |
|---|---|---|---|
| In general | Blade breakage | Poor practice | The blade must be efficient for the operation, material, and material thickness |
| | | Speed is wrong | Adjust for correct speed or stay as close as possible |
| | | Incorrect blade tension | Adjust tension for the blade and the operation |
| | | Forcing the cut | Allow the blade to cut at it's own pace |
| | | Blade twists | Don't force—don't turn corners too tight for the blade's width |
| | Sawed edge is bowed | Wrong tension | More tension usually helps |
| | | Wrong blade | Don't use very fine blades to saw thick stock |
| | Hard to follow line | Misalignment | Blade guide and backup might need adjustment |
| | | Blade guide not in line | Read owner's manual for adjustment procedure |
| | | Poor practice | Don't force the cut—feed slowly—accuracy is more important than speed |
| | | Wrong blade tension | Adjust for blade and operation |
| | Cutting action too slow | Blade teeth too fine | Change to better blade for material and material thickness |
| | | Dull blade | Discard |
| | | Hold-down too tight | Adjust for thickness of work |
| | | Speed (too slow?) | Increase speed for efficient cutting |
| | Cut edge not square | Misalignment | Adjust for 90 degrees angle between blade and table |

*Fig. 4-57.* Troubleshooting chart for the scroll saw.

| | The problem | Possible causes | What to check for or do |
|---|---|---|---|
| | Work lifts from table | Hold-down spring not set correctly | Adjust for light pressure down on the stock |
| | Vibration—chatter | Excessive speed | Adjust to correct speed |
| | | Setting of hold-down spring not correct | Check and adjust for stock thickness |
| | Sawdust not blown from cutting line | Air tube clogged | Remove and clean |
| | | Tube is kinked | Repair or replace |
| | | Blower mechanism at fault | Read manual for repair procedure |
| Metal sawing | Edges bend—excessive burring | No support at cutting area | Make special insert or back up work with scrap wood |
| | Blade teeth break—wear too quickly | Wrong blade or speed | Select better blade—adjust to more efficient speed |
| | Rough edges | Blade too coarse | Try finer, more suitable blade |
| | | No backup | Try special insert or scrap wood support for work |
| Sawing plastics | Kerf closes—binds blade | Poor practice | Use correct blade and speed |
| | Plastic marred | Poor practice | Keep, or apply, protective paper on plastic when sawing |
| Bevel cutting | Parts do not mesh | Poor practice | Wrong bevel angle—study text for correct procedure |
| Saber sawing | Hard to saw accurately | Wrong blade | Use special blades or heaviest jigsaw blade |
| | | Forcing cut | Feed slowly and guide carefully |
| | | Inadequate blade support | Read owner's manual for correct procedure |

| | The problem | Possible causes | What to check for or do |
|---|---|---|---|
| Filing— sanding | Sandpaper or files clog too quickly | Wrong speed | Usually too fast—slow to more suitable speed |
| | | Forcing | Ease up—allow sandpaper or file to cut at designed pace |

*Fig. 4-57.* Continued.

# Chapter 5

# Piercing

PIERCING IS AN EXCLUSIVE FUNCTION OF THE SCROLL SAW. NO OTHER MACHINE ALLOWS full exploitation of the technique. A portable saber saw can do a degree of piercing because it grips blades only at one end, but the comparatively wide blades it must function with don't permit the intricate cutting that is possible with a scroll saw. The band saw, if shop equipment allows breaking blades and then welding a new connection after they have been threaded through the stock, also can do some piercing. The kind of sawing that's possible is limited by the blade widths the machine can handle.

Piercing is internal cutting—forming openings through workpieces without having to enter from an edge of the stock. The method is possible on the scroll saw because the blade can be passed through a hole that is drilled through the material before it is installed. Thereafter, sawing is done in routine fashion (Figs. 5-1 and 5-2).

A blade entry hole must be drilled for each opening that the project requires. The intricacy of the project, or lack of it, dictates how many times you must stop sawing to resituate the blade. Just four holes were needed for the work going on in Fig. 5-3. The frame project that is detailed in Fig. 5-4 requires about a dozen. Even that is not excessive when compared with types of fret work that have dozens and dozens of small openings so that project seems to have more air than solid material. On the other hand, there are projects, like the one shown in Fig. 5-5, where a single blade insertion will suffice despite the intricate sawing that is needed to form the antlers.

For each opening, it is necessary to release the blade tension, loosen the blade clamp, pass the blade through the entry hole, secure the blade again, and then resupply tension. The procedure is less time consuming on some saws than others.

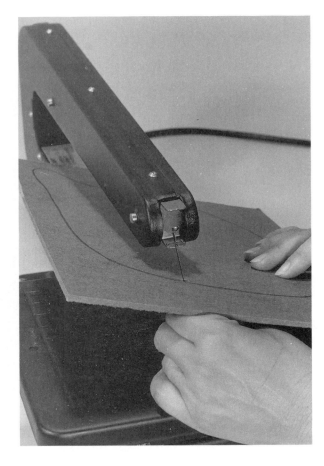

*Fig. 5-1.* Piercing, making internal cutouts without the need of a lead-in cut from an edge of the stock, is possible on the scroll saw because blades can be threaded through the material before they are mounted in the machine. (Dremel Photo.)

When blades have pivoting mounts, it's a matter of releasing the top clamp and then pivoting the blade forward so it can be threaded through the hole. On fixed-arm saws it might be necessary to release the blade at both ends. In some cases, when the blade is slim enough, and work thickness permits it, it's possible to flex the blade enough so it can pass through the hole without being released from the bottom clamp. The size of the entry hole is also a factor (Fig. 5-6).

## SIZING ENTRY HOLES

The diameter of the hole you drill for the blade depends primarily on the design of the project. It doesn't hurt to be generous whenever possible. In some situations, where it is necessary to start sawing in an acute corner, the entry hole should be barely enough to accommodate the blade (Figs. 5-7 and 5-8).

Entry holes, small or large, often can be used to supply part of the design and, in some cases, to facilitate sawing. Often, both motives are involved. Some of the holes that were predrilled in the horse project shown in Fig. 5-7 are used as entry

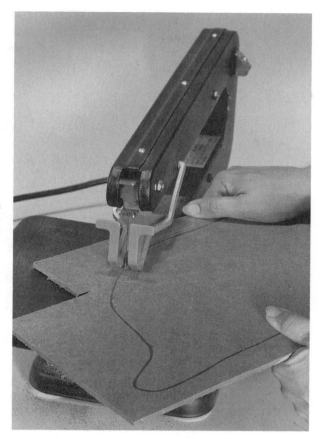

*Fig.* *5-2.* After the blade is installed and the work is positioned, sawing is done in a routine fashion. (Dremel Photo.)

holes, but they also supply nicely rounded corners. Figure 5-9 demonstrates how holes of a particular size that is suitable for the project become part of the design while also serving as entry holes for piercing.

Consider these two factors: If the scroll saw will only work with pin-type blades, then the smallest entry hole you can use must allow for the length of the pin in the blade. Blades that are premounted in clamps off the machine can't be used as is unless the entry hole is large enough to accommodate the clamps.

## SAWING

Piercing can be simple or complex, but in all cases it's wise to study the job before sawing so you can judge where to start for easiest work handling and the least amount of backtracking. The example in Fig. 5-10 is a very elementary chore but it does make a point. To produce the cutout in a continuous pass it's necessary to make a pivot turn at each of the corners. This can be done with a regular or spiral blade, but great care is required to keep the corners sharp.

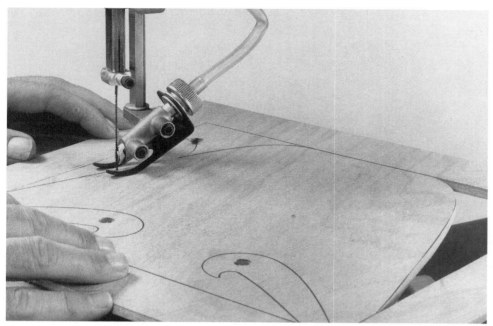

*Fig. 5-3.* An entry hole for the blade is drilled in each of the areas that will be cut out. This project required only four holes.

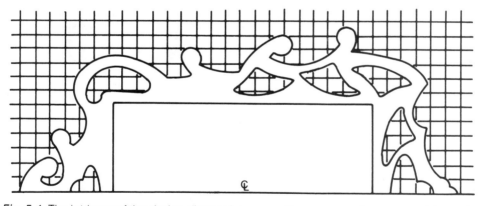

*Fig. 5-4.* The intricacy of the design dictates how many times you must remove and then reinstall the blade. This frame project requires that the chore be done a dozen times.

An alternate method is shown in Fig. 5-11. The first, continuous pass removes the bulk of the waste stock. Two additional cuts are required at the corners to remove remaining waste. You must retreat from one of the cuts so you can approach the second one. Another way to go is suggested in Fig. 5-12. The backtracking that is required is not more than is needed for the method that was shown in Fig. 5-11, but the sawing that is required to remove the remaining waste is just a single cut at each corner.

*Fig. 5-5.* This project, even though forming the antlers involves intricate sawing, needs only a single blade insertion hole.

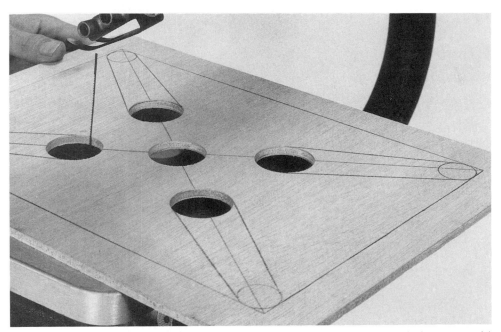

*Fig. 5-6.* The larger the entry hole, the easier it is to thread the blade. Large holes are an aid when piercing is done on a fixed-arm machine.

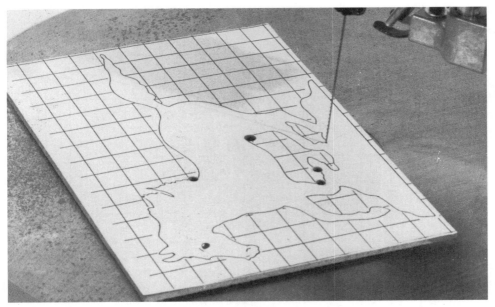

*Fig. 5-7.* Entry holes that just about accommodate the blade are used when sawing starts at an acute point or in a strictly confined area.

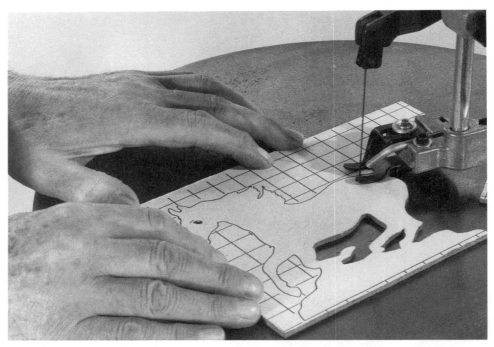

*Fig. 5-8.* Whether to do piercing first and then outline cuts is arbitrary. A thought that relates to size of the project is that doing outline cuts first reduces the material you can hold when doing the piercing.

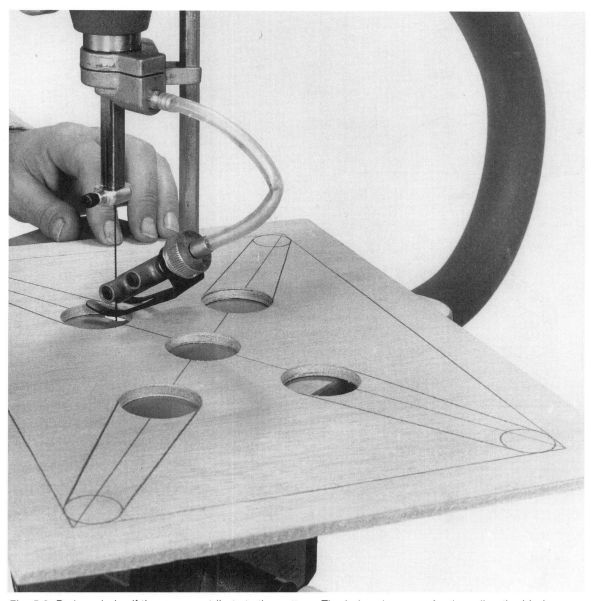

*Fig. 5-9.* Prebore holes if they can contribute to the pattern. The holes also serve for threading the blade.

## PSEUDO PIERCING

A project can often have the appearance of pierced work when it is actually an assembly of parts that were cut in normal fashion. Figure 5-13 shows an example of what can be done. The idea is by no means a substitute for the technique of piercing, but it can be useful. If, to prove the point, you saw a pattern through two pieces

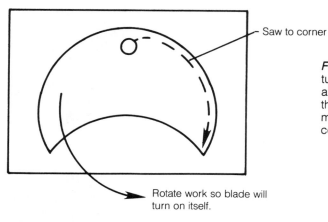

Saw to corner

Rotate work so blade will turn on itself.

Fig. 5-10. On this cutout, pivot turns at each of the corners allows a single pass to remove the waste. The pivot turning must be done precisely for the corners to be sharp.

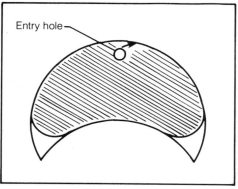

Entry hole

Make continuous cuts to remove bulk of waste (shaded)—then then make two cuts to clean out each corner.

Fig. 5-11. Some backtracking is required if the job is done this way. But avoiding pivot turning might make it easier to achieve sharp corners.

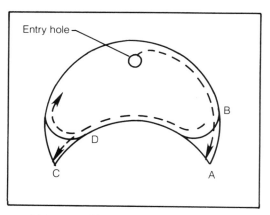

Entry hole

B

D

C

A

Make cut to "A," backtrack to "B" and proceed to "C"—backtrack to "D" and return to start point. Single cut at each corner will remove remaining waste.

Fig. 5-12. Another way to work. This sawing method requires a minimum of backtracking.

*Fig. 5-13.* Pieces that have been pad-sawed and then joined edge-to-edge will appear as a solid piece that has been produced by piercing. Think of the waste as possible components for other projects.

that have been joined as a pad and then, after inverting one piece, glue them edge-to-edge, you will have what appears to be pierced work. The joint is important. The less obvious it is, the more the project will seem to have been cut from a single piece. The number of duplicates you can produce depends on the plies that are in the pad.

## UNIQUE USES FOR PIERCING

Piercing can be done through adjacent sides of stock so the result is a hollow in the material. The example shown in Fig. 5-14 was scroll sawed in such fashion and then turned to shape in a lathe. The piercing can be done after the part is turned if the project has flat areas so it can be placed without problems on the scroll-saw table. The idea does not have to be restricted to lathe turnings. It is necessary, of course, that the dimensions of the stock do not exceed the depth-of-cut capacity of the saw.

*Fig. 5-14.* Piercing through adjacent sides of base stock can result in interesting hollows. This example ended as a lathe project but the technique has other applications.

# Chapter 6

# Compound Angle Sawing

COMPOUND ANGLE SAWING IS AN OPERATION THAT INVOLVES SAWING PATTERNS ON ADJAcent sides of the stock. It's not possible to read anything about a band saw that doesn't use the cabriole leg as an example of what can be produced by the technique. The band saw, because of its great depth of cut, can be more flexible in this area, but only in project size. The scroll saw can emulate the procedures as long as the workpiece is within the tool's capacity. Actually, the scroll saw can go a step farther. For example, piercing operations can be done before or after the initial sawing to add embellishments, something not possible on the band saw.

Craftspeople who do bas-relief work or carving in the round often will do compound sawing to create a basic form before going to work with other tools. The same thought applies to lathe enthusiasts. Turning is reduced to actual shaping when the bulk of the waste material is removed by presawing.

## LAYOUT

The first step is to draw a full-size pattern of the project. It can be drawn directly on the workpiece or on paper attached to the stock. Outlines on paper can be positioned on each side of a fold line that will facilitate accurate placement on the stock (Fig. 6-1). A better idea is to provide the pattern on stiff cardboard that you cut as a template for marking the workpiece or for transferring to paper. The motive is to have a permanent pattern for future use.

Twin patterns are not always the way to go. For example, the whale project that is shown in Figs. 6-2 and 6-3 requires one pattern for the side view and a different one

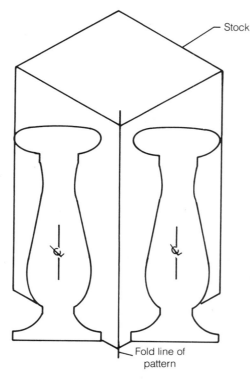

Stock

Fold line of
pattern

*Fig. 6-1.* Compound angle sawing requires that patterns be drawn on adjacent sides of the workpiece. Whether the patterns are twins or dissimilar depends on the design of the project.

for the top. When placing or tracing dissimilar patterns, mark centerlines on adjacent sides of the workpiece as guides for aligning the two views. The fold method that was shown in Fig. 6-1 is also applicable.

## SAWING

The cabriole leg, if sized within the limits of the machine, provides an effective way to demonstrate compound angle sawing. It also is a good shape for practicing and understanding the technique.

The first step—after the workpiece is marked—is to determine which side to saw first. A decision is based on how many pieces will be cut away during the initial sawing, because pieces that are sawed off must be returned to original positions for the second step. The fewer pieces there are, the less troublesome final sawing will be. Actually, for most projects, this isn't terribly critical, but it does no harm to check.

Figure 6-4 shows the first steps for sawing the cabriole leg. The first cut was a straight one to the top of the curve. After backtracking, the piece was turned end-for-end so the waste could be removed in a single piece. The next cut completes the initial operation.

Before final sawing can be done, the released pieces must be returned so the stock will again be "solid" and have a flat surface for placing on the saw's table. You can reattach the cutoffs with tape as long as enough is used to ensure the assembly

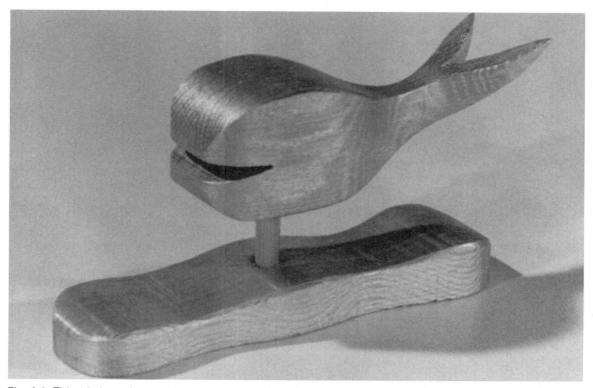

*Fig. 6-2.* This whale project requires two patterns. The view from the side is not the same as that from the top.

*Fig. 6-3.* Side- and top-view patterns that can be used for the whale project. For a larger project, just enlarge the size of the squares. More information on patterns and layout will be provided in chapter 11.

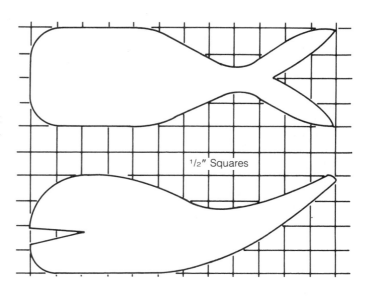

1/2" Squares

*Fig. 6-4.* First sawing steps for the cabriole leg. It's wise to plan for the least number of cutoffs.

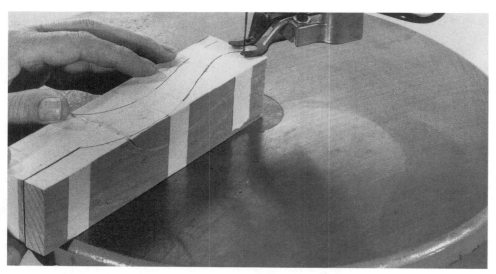

*Fig. 6-5.* The final sawing chores are done on the adjacent side of the workpiece after parts have been reassembled as a solid block.

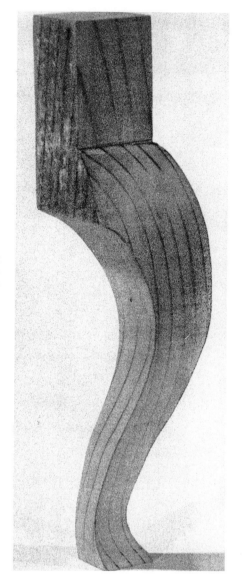

*Fig. 6-6.* The form of the project appears after sawing is complete and all waste parts have been removed.

won't fall apart as you saw. You can use double-faced tape, or even small nails, if you are careful to avoid placing them on a cut line.

When the project is ready, sawing the second side imitates the steps followed the first time (Fig. 6-5). The project is revealed after sawing is completed and the waste pieces have been removed (Fig. 6-6).

Compound angle sawing is an intriguing application, and practical for producing components or semifinished projects. The ideas shown in Figs. 6-7 and 6-8 are typical projects where the technique is used to provide the basic form.

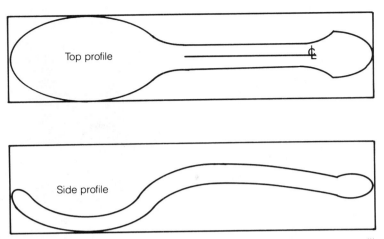

Top profile

Side profile

*Fig. 6-7.* Compound angle sawing is used to provide the basic form for projects like this.

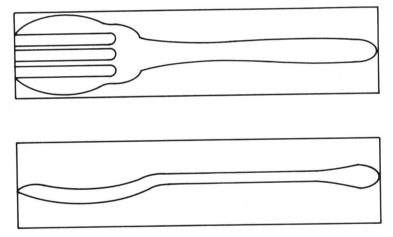

*Fig. 6-8.* The "fork," which should be about twice as large as the pattern shows, is another typical project that is easier to accomplish if compound sawing is used to provide the basic form.

# Chapter 7

# Bevel Sawing

I TALKED SOME ABOUT BEVEL SAWING IN CHAPTER 4, WHICH DISCUSSED STRAIGHT CUTS that were made at an angle through the thickness of the stock by working with the tool's table tilted. The type of bevel sawing that will be covered in this chapter is totally different. This technique enables the operator to, among other things, form a deep bowl from a single flat board. A standby procedure for a deep project calls for bevel-sawing concentric rings with diminishing inside and outside diameters, but cut from separate pieces of wood. The rings are then assembled as shown in Fig. 7-1. The bevel angle is constant; the difference between inside and outside diameters determines the thickness of the walls.

## MAKING DEEP PROJECTS FROM A SINGLE BOARD

The special technique also involves bevel sawing concentric rings, but from a single board. When important rules are followed, each ring will jam tightly into the piece it was cut from (Fig. 7-2). Figure 7-3 illustrates how the idea works. If you saw a disc in the center of a workpiece with the table in normal position, the disc will pass through the opening. Do the same thing, but with the table tilted to a particular angle and the beveled disc will fall only part way through the beveled opening; it will jam into place. Cut a series of beveled rings with a common center and the result is a cone shape after each ring has been jammed into the opening it was cut from. The more rings, the deeper the project.

How far the rings project, which, in total, determines the depth of the project, will depend on the thickness of the stock, the bevel angle, and the width of the kerf (Fig. 7-4). If, for example, you cut six concentric rings in a board that is 3/4-inch thick and

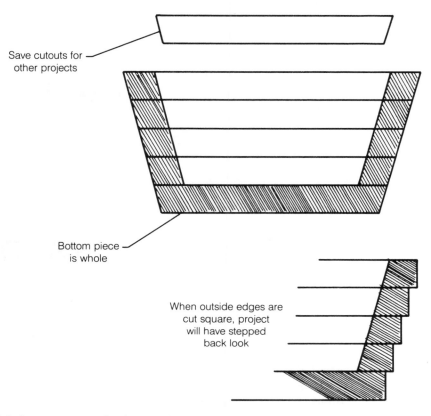

Save cutouts for
other projects

Bottom piece
is whole

When outside edges are
cut square, project
will have stepped
back look

*Fig. 7-1.* A common practice for creating deep projects is to bevel saw concentric rings that diminish in size. Each ring is cut from a separate piece of stock.

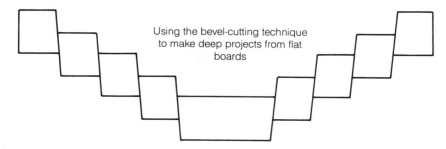

Using the bevel-cutting technique
to make deep projects from flat
boards

*Fig. 7-2.* The bevel-sawing technique also involves sawing concentric rings, but all rings are cut from a single piece of material.

6-inches square, and each ring projects $1/2$ inch, the assembled parts will measure $3^1/4$ inches high and 6 inches across.

The less table tilt that you use, the greater the projection of each individual piece will be. The greater the number of pieces that are sawed, the more the total projection. It's difficult, at times, to determine beforehand the exact projection that will

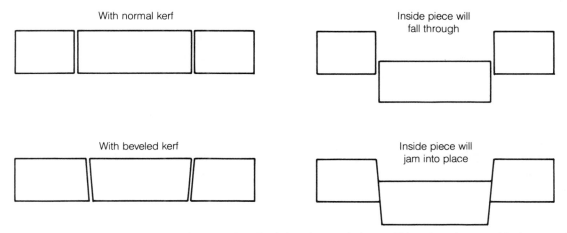

*Fig. 7-3.* Why the bevel-sawing technique works. Each bevel-sawed piece will jam into the opening it was cut from. Slight bevel angles result in maximum projection, but also in thin wall sections.

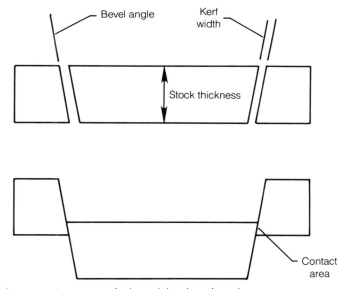

*Fig. 7-4.* The factors to be aware of when doing bevel sawing.

result. So, to get started toward acceptable results, it pays to make a single trial cut in a sample of the material and measure it. It's important to know that if you use a minimum table tilt to get maximum projection, the project will have a thin wall thickness. This will make it difficult to do a good job of gluing the rings together. Also, a thin wall thickness makes it difficult to avoid fractures when doing any necessary follow-up operations, such as smoothing inside and outside surfaces.

## TABLE TILTS

In my own experiences I have found that a table tilt of two to five degrees works pretty well on materials from 1/4-inch to 3/4-inch thick as long as the blade doesn't form a heavy kerf. As a starting point, a blade that has about 15 teeth per inch (TPI) and is .020 thick × .110 wide is as good a blade as any to "play" with. Figures 7-5 and 7-6 supply an indication of projections that will occur when different bevel angles are used on various material thicknesses.

While minimum bevel angles will provide maximum projection, working toward minimum projection by using greater bevel angles can lead to interesting effects, such as the sample shown in Fig. 7-7. The pattern will be slightly recessed, or appear in relief, depending on which side of the project will be exposed.

Another factor of bevel sawing, one that is especially useful when producing solid wood inlays, is detailed in Figs. 7-8 and 7-9. When two parts are sawed as a pad, opposing pieces can be brought together tightly enough to eliminate the kerf. Some experimenting might be in order to determine the right combination of table tilt and blade in relation to the thickness of the material.

## ENTRY HOLES

The category of bevel sawing that we have been discussing involves piercing applications (chapter 5). Normally, the entry hole for the blade is drilled squarely through the stock. When bevel sawing, the hole must be drilled at an angle that matches the tilt of the table. The chore will be easy if a drill press is handy because its table can be

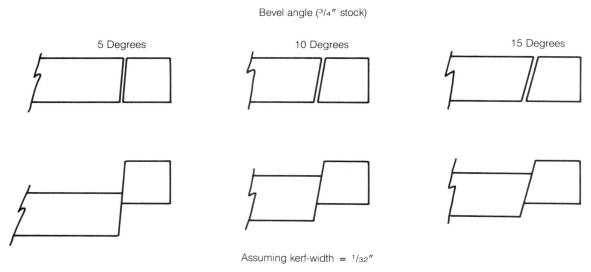

Bevel angle (3/4" stock)

5 Degrees  10 Degrees  15 Degrees

Assuming kerf-width = 1/32"

*Fig. 7-5.* Some idea of the projections that will occur when bevel sawing 3/4-inch stock at various angles. Note how the contact area between rings increases as more bevel angle is used.

On 2″ stock—bevel angle = 2¹/₂ degrees

¹/₃₂″ Kerf

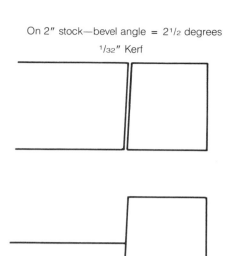

*Fig. 7-6.* A 2¹/₂-degree bevel angle on 2-inch stock will result in acceptable projection and contact area. The contact area is what will determine the wall thickness of the project.

*Fig. 7-7.* Minimum projection can result in interesting effects. The cutout will be slightly recessed on one side of the base stock, and will appear in relief on the opposite side.

tilted to the angle that is needed. When the job is done with a hand or portable electric drill, it's a good idea to supply an angle gauge that can be done simply by sawing a small piece of ³/₄-inch stock at the necessary angle.

How many holes are needed will depend on the project. A single hole for a disc; X-number of holes if the work involves multiple, concentric rings (Figs. 7-10 and 7-11). As always, the size of the holes should be barely enough to permit threading the blade. Tiny holes will be easy to conceal by filling them with wood dough after the project has been assembled.

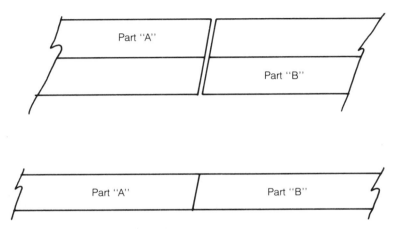

*Fig. 7-8.* When opposing pieces of a two-piece pad that has been bevel sawed are put together, the pieces will mate with a hardly visible joint line.

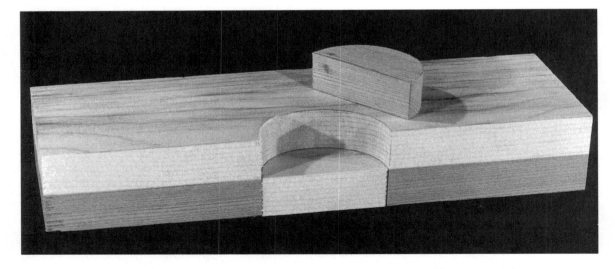

*Fig. 7-9.* The top cutout in this bevel-sawed pad will fit tightly in the bottom layer. The two remaining components will not fit the same way.

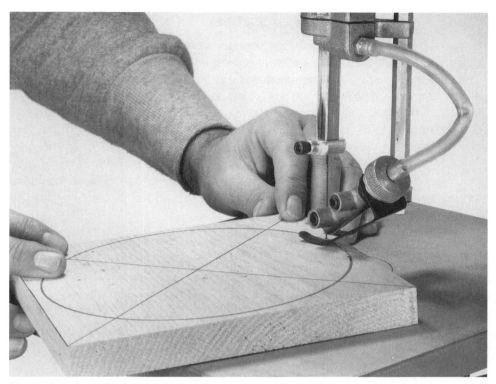

*Fig. 7-10.* A single blade-insertion hole is all that is needed when a single disc is bevel sawed.

*Fig. 7-11.* Entry holes must be drilled to match the tilt angle of the table. Be careful to stay on line when sawing. The entry holes can be used to orient pieces at assembly time.

## ASSEMBLY

Because bevel-sawed parts jam together, assembling can be accomplished without clamps. Use glue on mating edges and press interior parts into place. Be careful with placement, especially when multiple rings are involved. If you don't ensure that all components will be horizontal, the project as a whole will tilt. Don't be overly generous with glue because the idea is to have a minimum amount that is squeezed out of the joints and must be cleaned off. Do the cleaning with a damp, lint-free cloth as soon as parts are joined.

Sometimes, it's wise to supply additional reinforcement. The project, for example, might be a base for a lamp or heavy vase whose weight will bear on the projecting piece. In such cases, small glue blocks can be added to the assembly (Fig. 7-12).

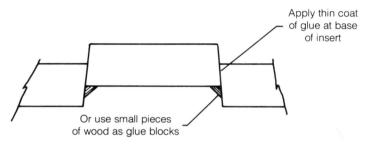

*Fig. 7-12.* Small glue blocks can be used as reinforcement when the projecting piece must support some weight.

## TYPICAL APPLICATIONS

Creating blanks for lathe turnings is one of the intriguing ways to put bevel sawing to good use (Fig. 7-13). The method can be used just to save material, or can provide a solution when you have a board of exotic wood that isn't available in a turning-blank size that you would like to have for the project.

Before you create the blank, you must consider all the factors that will affect the assembly, especially providing for a suitable wall thickness that allows using lathe chisels without cutting through. The best way is to draw a full-size layout of a cross section of the blank and then sketch in the contours that you will shape (Figs. 7-14 and 7-15). Making test bevel cuts in scrap material, not necessarily from the project wood, but something of equal thickness, will help you plan the way to go.

## CHANGES IN CONTOURS

So far, bevel-sawing techniques have been illustrated by circular cutting, but the idea is just as useful when the shape of the project requires changes in the contour of the cut. A hollow, model boat hull provides a good example of how the method can be used for more than bowl shapes.

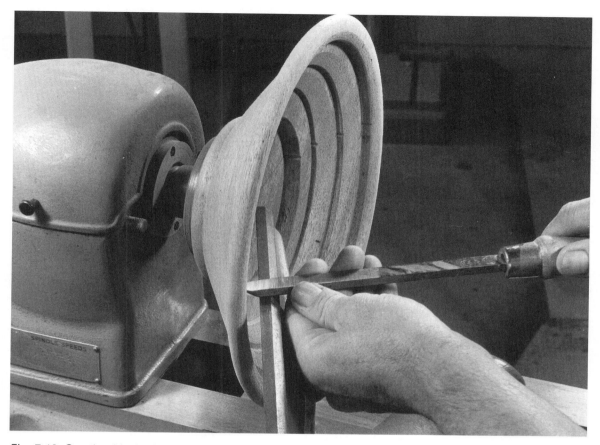

*Fig. 7-13.* Creating blanks for lathe turning is one of the most practical and impressive applications for bevel sawing. The material for this 12-inch-diameter bowl was supplied by a single piece of ³/₄-inch × 12-inches-square stock.

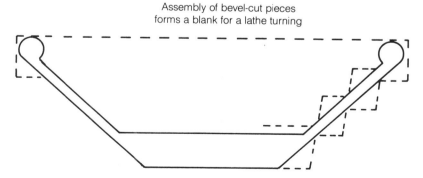

Assembly of bevel-cut pieces
forms a blank for a lathe turning

*Fig. 7-14.* Draw a full-size cross-sectional view of the project so you can determine the bevel angle that will provide an acceptable wall thickness.

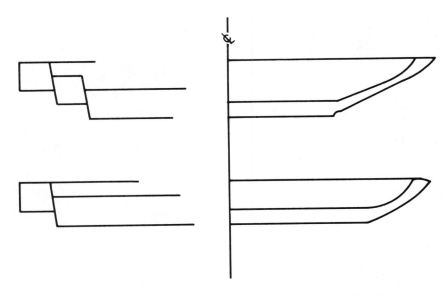

*Fig. 7-15*. A few layers of material can supply what is needed for projects like shallow bowls and trays.

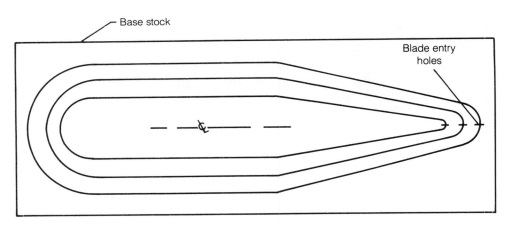

Base stock

Blade entry holes

*Fig. 7-16*. Typical top-view layout of a hollow boat hull. Be sure, when sawing, to maintain a constant relationship between blade and work. If you swing the work in the wrong direction, the direction of the bevel will change and the parts will not fit.

The first step is to provide a full-size top view of the project with lines that indicate the cut paths (Fig. 7-16). It's also a good idea to follow the preliminary layout suggestions that were made for lathe turnings. That is, draw a full-size cross section of the project so you can preview wall thickness. Sawing is done in normal fashion but, as with all bevel sawing, it is critical that the work have the same relationship with the blade throughout the sawing operations. If this changes, so will the direction of the bevel and the components won't fit.

Final shaping of the hull is done by hand after the parts are assembled. The bulk of the waste can be removed with rasps or sharp chisels; the last smoothing with sandpaper (Figs. 7-17 through 7-19).

## NUMBERS AND LETTERS

Bevel sawing provides the opportunity to produce signs or house numbers. These figures gain more prominence by projecting or recessing from a surface (Fig. 7-20). The result will depend on which side of the base stock the project will be viewed

*Fig. 7-17.* The hull will look like this after the sawed components have been assembled.

*Fig. 7-18.* Outside surfaces are then shaped by working with rasps or chisels.

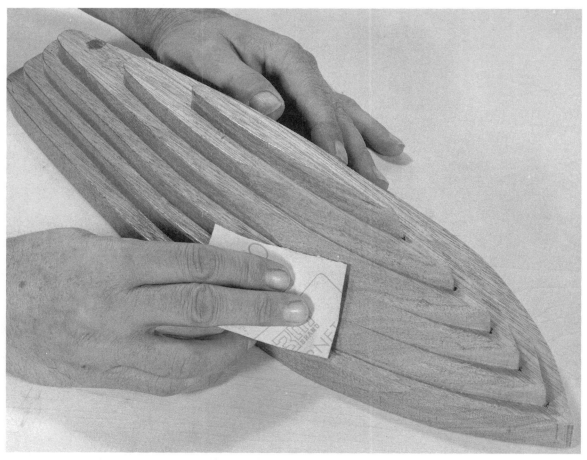

*Fig. 7-19.* Do one small section as a test so you will know how much material you can remove without fracturing the hull.

from. If the example project is turned end-for-end so the projection side of the figures would be apparent, then the numbers would appear in reverse order. There is no problem if the project can be viewed from one side or the other without manipulation. One view will show projecting figures; the other, recessed figures.

It's wise when doing work of this nature to avoid letter or number designs like those shown in Fig. 7-21. It's not that they can't be cut, only that the great number of sharp pivot turns that are needed add significantly to the care required to do the project successfully.

Letters or numbers with beveled edges that slant in a common direction can be formed only with a spiral blade (Fig. 7-22). The reason is that a spiral blade will cut in any direction. Sawing occurs whether the workpiece is moved left or right, or forward or back; it does not have to be rotated to keep the blade on the pattern line. Thus, the

*Fig. 7-20.* Bevel-sawed numbers (or letters) are more prominent if they are recessed or allowed to project. These numbers were painted before assembly. The openings through numbers eight and six were supplied by drilling.

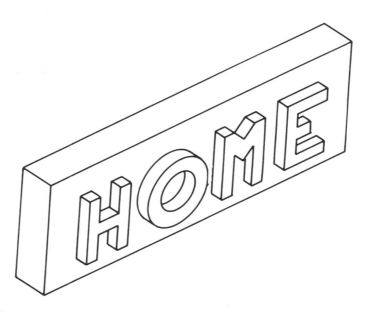

*Fig. 7-21.* Figures that are designed this way, with many sharp corners, require many abrupt pivot turns. Sawing will be easier if rounded corners are used instead of square ones.

bevel on one side of a figure will parallel the bevel on the opposite side. For example, bevel sawing with a conventional blade where the workpiece must be rotated will form a figure like the one shown in Fig. 7-23. With a spiral blade, where work rotation is not a factor, results can be like the example shown in Fig. 7-24.

*Fig. 7-22.* Projects like this, where all planes of the figures slant in a common direction, can be done with spiral blades, not with conventional ones.

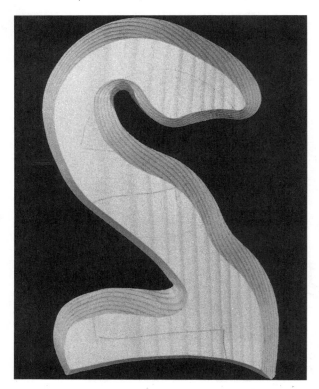

*Fig. 7-23.* When sawing with a conventional blade, the work must be rotated to keep the blade on the line. Thus, bevel angles on opposite sides slant in different directions.

Fig. 7-24. When a spiral blade that can cut in any direction is used, the workpiece does not have to be rotated, so the bevels can parallel each other.

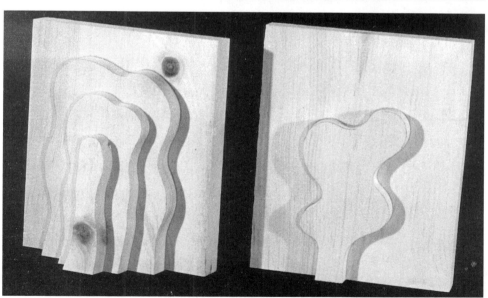

Fig. 7-25. Examples of bevel cutting that were done without following a specific pattern.

## FUN WITH BEVEL SAWING

It's often enjoyable to be a bit daring with techniques that were invented for particular applications. Bevel sawing, as I discovered in the shop on a day when I had no special project in mind but had the urge to do some scroll sawing, is one of them. Figures 7-25 and 7-26 show what emerged from the fun time.

No special sawing procedures are required. Work with a reasonably fine blade and choose a table-tilt that results in acceptable projection. The idea is to forget a preplanned pattern and to follow imaginative lines that just seem to happen. After the first part is cut, use it as base stock to saw another design. This can be repeated

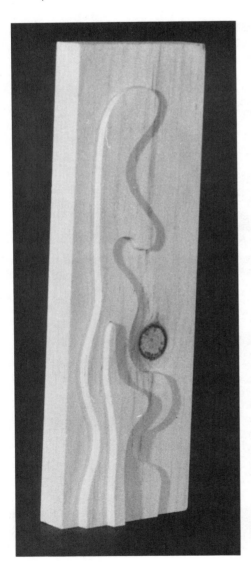

*Fig. 7-26.* Each cutout is viewed as base stock for additional sawing. Results can be surprisingly attractive.

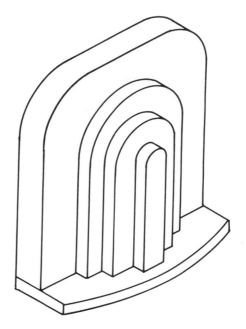

*Fig. 7-27.* Projects can have practical applications. This multiple bevel-cut workpiece, when fitted with a back and bottom, makes a dandy bookend.

several times until you find that the total projection and the appearance of the project pleases you. The projection of individual pieces can be varied simply by changing the bevel angle for each piece you cut.

It might happen that you will lack enthusiasm for some of the results, but this is one of those situations, where you "can't win them all." It also might happen that a result is so satisfying that you duplicate it in some exotic wood and display it as a decorative plaque.

There also can be practical uses for what you produce. Figure 7-27 offers a suggestion. Add a bottom and a back to the 3-D project and you have a bookend. To contribute some weight, fill the rear voids with some dry sand before attaching a back. Weight also can be increased by using plaster of paris. If you use plaster, first apply several coats of wood sealer to those surfaces that the plaster will contact.

# Chapter 8

# Inlay Work

THERE IS *INLAY WORK* AND THERE IS *MARQUETRY*, AND THE TERMS ARE OFTEN USED INTER-changeably. Marquetry derives from a French word meaning to "spot" or "mark;" to extend it a bit farther—"to mark with many colors." Wood has almost countless hues—from white to black—and craftspeople have taken advantage of this fact to produce designs and pictures by using pieces of wood of different species and color.

## DIFFERENCES BETWEEN INLAY WORK AND MARQUETRY

Inlay literally means to recess something so it will be flush with surrounding surfaces. The inlay can be a foreign material or it can be cut from the parent stock. If you saw a disc from a board and then replace it, or if you saw a shape from one piece and then set it in a matching recess carved in a second piece, then you have done inlay work. The latter technique is often called *intarsia* or mosaic woodwork.

Creating a design or picture that consists of X-number of pieces can be done in one of two ways. Inlaid pictures can be produced in quantity by using a normal blade angle to saw through a pad of veneers. Each piece from one ply will fit the corresponding opening in another ply. Four pieces of veneer? Four projects. There will be a visible kerf between pieces that must be filled after the parts are assembled.

True marquetry is done by bevel sawing two layers so that the cutout from one will fit the other but without a kerf. A method that is quite exacting is to saw pieces individually so all will fit perfectly without a visible kerf.

When sawing is done precisely, it takes a very close examination to reveal the method. Are the three examples that are shown in Figs. 8-1, 8-2, and 8-3, (courtesy of Constantine's) inlaid pictures or are they marquetry?

*Fig. 8-1.* Call it inlay or marquetry, projects like this are scroll-saw art. It takes time and careful sawing to produce them, but the results are worth it. Note how the grain direction of the background helps to point up the figure.

*Fig. 8-2.* Careful selection of wood species and color are important first steps. In this production, colors are mostly either black or white.

*Fig. 8-3.* Intricate sawing is needed to bring out features. Note the tiny highlight in the eyes.

## REVIEWING SAWING METHODS

When sawing is done with a 90-degree angle between the blade and the table, the cutout will be outlined by the width of the kerf (Fig. 8-4). The control you have is in the selection of the blade that will saw efficiently. The kerf in veneers can be almost negligible because you can work with extremely fine blades. Actually, you should experiment with fine blades even in thicker stock, choosing the finest one that will get the job done.

When the work is done by bevel sawing a two-piece pad, the cutout from one piece will fit "kerfless" in the corresponding opening of the second piece (Fig. 8-5 and 8-6). The remaining pieces are considered waste because they can't be put together as precisely as the project parts (Fig. 8-7). However, there is no reason why you can't make use of them by gluing them to a backing, leaving the kerf as is or filling it with wood dough.

## THE PAD METHOD

The first step is to make a selection of wood veneers of contrasting colors. This takes some consideration because you must visualize how the contrasts will point up the

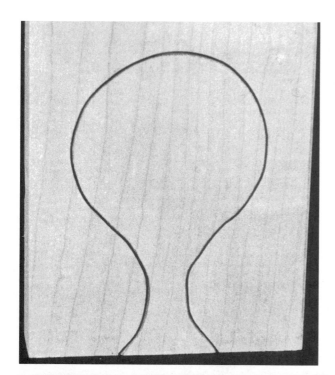

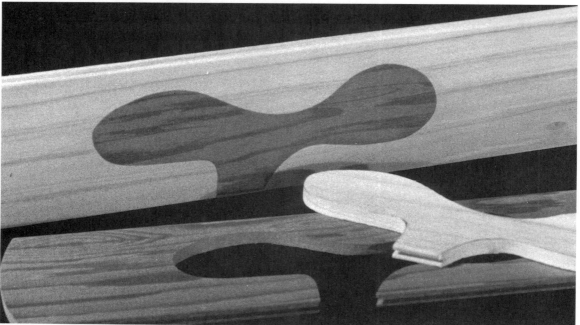

*Fig. 8-4.* When the sawing is done with blade and table in normal position, the inlay will be outlined by the width of the kerf.

*Fig. 8-5.* Bevel sawing a two-piece pad will result in a flush, tight-fitting inlay. Some experimenting might be required to determine the best blade and the right bevel angle for the job.

*Fig. 8-6.* All projects will be successful if you remember to always keep the work, or cut if you prefer, on the same side of the blade. If you do otherwise, the direction of the bevel will change and the parts will not fit.

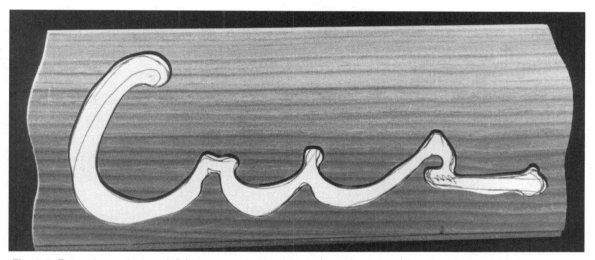

*Fig. 8-7.* Extra pieces that are left from a bevel-sawed, two-ply pad are considered waste because they can't go together like the project components. But, if you don't mind the kerf . . . ?

picture. If you are working from an illustration you can take your cue from its colors. If the design is original, then mark areas to indicate particular tones and grain direction of various pieces.

Veneers are delicate and must be handled carefully. It's possible that some veneers have wrinkled areas when you buy them. If you try to flatten them without taking some precautions, you might cause cracks. It is better to dampen the veneer pieces a bit with a lint-free cloth and press them between pieces of plywood and a weight a day or two before you plan to use them.

The design you plan to saw can be pasted or drawn on a top layer of veneer, but you will have better control if the pad is sandwiched between top and bottom layers of thin hardboard or thick posterboard. A good way to assemble the pad is to tape the plies to each other and to the covers. The covers will keep the pad flat and also will serve to eliminate any feathering that can occur while sawing. Don't assemble a pad that is more than 1/4-inch thick, not to start with anyway.

Start sawing at some interior point. This involves piercing to start with, and more might be required, but if you start with interior openings, you might find that the need for piercing will be minimized. Use a very fine blade (experienced workers will often use jewelers blades) and, if the machine allows, a slow speed. Because you are sawing with the table set 90 degrees to the blade, you can move the work in any direction to keep the blade on the pattern line.

As you release pieces from the pad, place them on a surface in their relative positions. After sawing is complete, you decide which piece from which ply is best suited for joining to an adjacent piece from another ply. Assuming there were four pieces of veneer in the pad, you will end up with four inlays that are ready for final assembly.

Place the pieces face up and hold them together with gummed tape. A special veneer tape is available for this purpose and it is wise to have some, especially for large projects. I have found that on more simple chores, ordinary masking tape will serve (Fig. 8-8). Now is not the time to be concerned about kerfs. They will be filled in later.

*Fig. 8-8.* After sawing is done for an inlay project, mating parts are joined with tape. The tape is applied to the face side of the veneers. It is a good idea to tape over all kerfs.

The next step is to attach the assembly, tape-side up, to a solid backing. This can be done with regular or veneer glue, or even contact cement. Peel off the tape after the glue is dry. If there is a problem, use a damp rag to moisten the tape. This will help to soften the tape adhesive, but don't use so much water that you soak the veneers.

The final step is to do some very light sanding and then to fill the kerfs with thin wood dough. It's possible to use a neutral wood filler over the entire project. This will fill the kerfs and any open pores that might be characteristic of some of the veneers that were used. When all work is done, you will have multiple inlays, each one a copy of the others, but different because of the various veneers that were used to make the pad (Fig. 8-9).

## NONWOOD INLAYS

Inlay projects do not have to be all wood. Often, metals such as brass, copper, or aluminum or even precious metals such as gold or silver are used.

Figure 8-10 shows an aluminum candlestick profile inlayed in a background of mahogany plywood. Because the project was done by bevel sawing, the extra pieces, those in the foreground of the illustration, are considered waste. Because metal is involved, projects like this are done best with metal piercing blades.

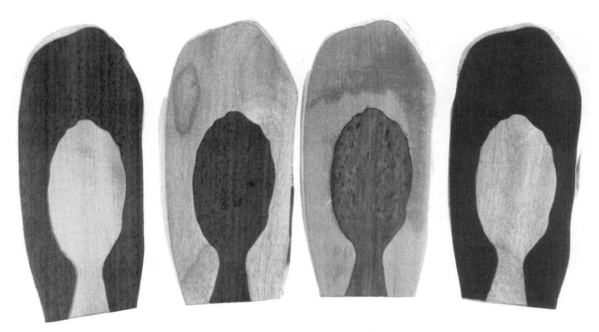

*Fig. 8-9.* Pad sawing results in multiple inlays. Each project is a twin of another, yet different because of contrasting woods and colors.

*Fig. 8-10.* Doing inlays by combining metal and wood can lead to interesting projects. Bevel sawing was used here; materials are aluminum and mahogany plywood. The pieces in the foreground are ''waste.'' This type of sawing should be done with a metal piercing (jewelers) blade.

## SOLID WOOD INLAYS

Solid wood inlays can be produced by sawing normally or by using the two-ply bevel sawing idea. When the cut is square and an open kerf is part of the picture, it can be filled to blend with adjacent areas. Another idea is to fill the kerf with a contrasting wood dough instead of trying to hide it. Making the most of the ''flaw'' will often provide interesting design details.

A similar thought that will add interest is to slightly chamfer all mating edges, or to set the inlay a bit below the surface of the background material (Figs. 8-11 and 8-12).

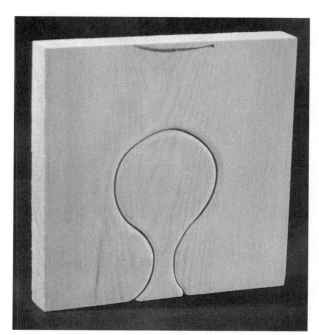

*Fig. 8-11.* Chamfering the edges of the background and the insert can make the kerf line part of the design.

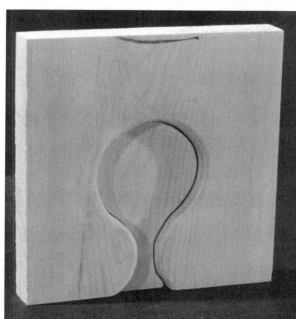

*Fig. 8-12.* Recessing the insert is another thought. The projection at the back can be sanded flush if necessary.

# Chapter 9

# Saber Sawing

**S**ABER SAWING (SOMETIMES SPELLED "SABRE") IS NOT THE FORTE OF THE SCROLL SAW nor is it possible to do this type of sawing on all machines. Blades must be clamped only at their lower ends, and to fully utilize the technique it should be possible to remove or swing down the upper arm of the tool (Fig. 9-1). This pretty much limits the application to fixed-arm designs like those offered by Delta and Shopsmith. The lower blade clamps on these machines are actually chucks that can grip heavy blades firmly and keep them in vertical position.

*Fig. 9-1.* The primary use for saber sawing is to make cuts on oversize workpieces. Move the work very carefully. Even though the blade is stiff and has some support under the table, it can bend and move off the pattern line. Provide outboard support when the work is large enough to be unwieldy.

## USING SCROLL AND SABER SAW BLADES

The heaviest of scroll saw blades, such as one that is 3/16 inch or 1/4 inch wide and has about 9 TPI, can be used for saber sawing (Fig. 9-2). It also is possible that blades designed for use in portable saber saws (now called jigsaws) can be used (Fig. 9-3). It depends on the stroke of the machine and the height of the table. There must be enough blade length working above the table for the idea to be practical.

*Fig. 9-2.* The largest scroll-saw blades can be used for saber sawing. They should be 3/16 inch to 1/4 inch wide and, especially when sawing thick stock, have few teeth per inch. Be sure to use the backup that is supplied under the table.

Routine saber sawing, even piercing, can be done without interference from the upper arm if the size of the workpiece allows it (Fig. 9-4). When working so, there is no reason why the tool's guides and hold-down can't be used even though the blade is not secured at its top end (Fig. 9-5).

Saber sawing requires very careful work handling to keep the blade from bending or moving off the pattern line even though stiff blades are used. Work slowly, and remember that, because of the blade widths that are usable, you can't make the intricate cuts or the sharp turns that are possible with narrow blades.

*Fig. 9-3.* Blades that are supplied for portable saber saws are also usable if blade stroke and table height allow enough of the blade to work above the table.

*Fig. 9-4.* Piercing on heavy stock also is a saber-sawing possibility. Keep the upper arm in place whenever the size of the work allows you to. Working with a blade that is gripped at only one end makes it easy to move from one insertion hole to another.

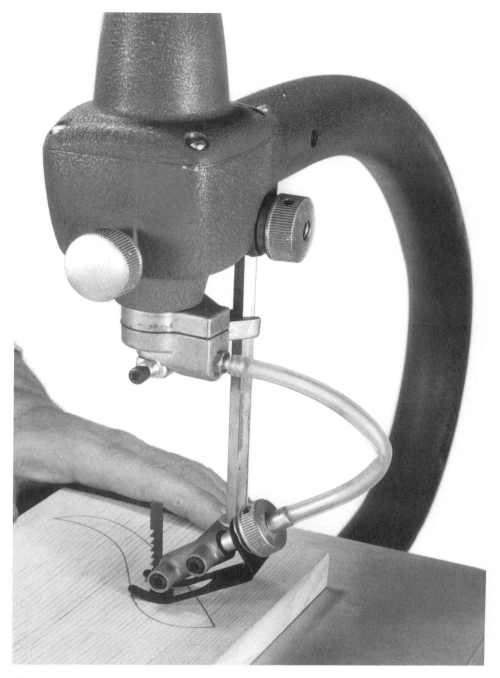

*Fig. 9-5.* When the arm can remain, use guides and hold-downs as you would for regular sawing. Because you can't make sharp turns with wide blades, making internal cutouts will usually require a lot of backtracking.

# Chapter 10

# Special Applications

ANYTHING YOU DO ON ANY POWER TOOL IS, REALLY, "SPECIAL," IF ONLY YOU CONSIDER the time and effort that is saved and how the tool helps you work more accurately. In this chapter I deal with applications that are sometimes innovative in terms of extending the scope of the machine, and other times a mechanical means of doing a routine job more conveniently or that provides a way to produce exact duplicates. You might not think of the scroll saw as a machine for forming joints, especially if other tools, such as a table saw and a portable router are available, but joint making and other thoughts are here for you to consider. Part of the fun of woodworking is inventing practical uses for the tool that even the manufacturer didn't think of. Being tool wise often leads to original thoughts that can solve unique problems.

## GUIDED CIRCULAR AND ARC SAWING

Circular sawing is a common procedure that calls for no particular finesse other than moving the work carefully so the blade will stay on the pattern line. Still, you can provide mechanical accuracy and be better equipped for producing multiple, similar pieces if you work with a pivot jig. The pivot jig shown mounted in Fig. 10-1 and detailed in Fig. 10-2, was made for the Delta scroll saw. With some minor modification of the way the jig is attached to the hold-down arm, the design can be adapted to other saws.

The post, which substitutes for the one on the machine, is a length of threaded steel rod that is ground or filed flat at its upper end so that the machine's lock screw or knob can bear firmly against it. The adjustable pivot is a machine screw that has a pointed end. The end can be shaped by rotating the screw against a grinding wheel or even a disc sander. If you cut off the head of the screw, which won't interfere with its function, you can chuck the screw in a drill press and hold a file against it to form the point, or grip it in a portable drill so you can spin its end against a turning grinding wheel.

You must consider two important factors when using the jig to saw true circles. The line between the pivot point and the blade must be perpendicular and the pivot

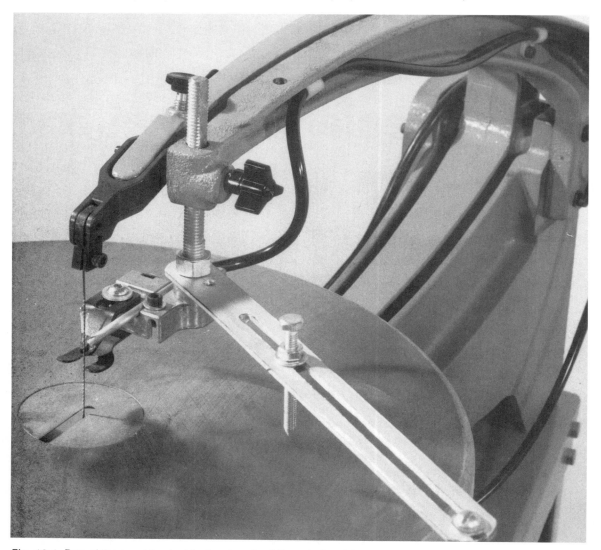

*Fig. 10-1.* Part of the topside pivot jig is a length of threaded rod that substitutes for the post normally used for mounting the tool's guides and hold-downs. The jig can be raised or lowered and swung in any direction for aligning the pivot point with the saw blade.

must be aligned with the points of the blade's teeth (Fig. 10-3). If you do not follow these rules the blade will wander off the circumference. It's also wise to use a blade that is in prime condition.

Sawing can start in one of two ways. The workpiece can be square with dimensions that match the diameter of the circle. In this case, the cut is started by placing

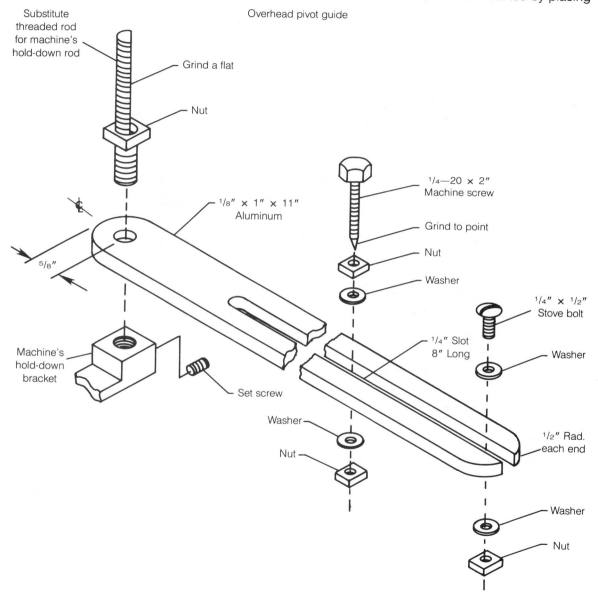

*Fig. 10-2.* These are the parts required for the pivot jig. Some changes might be needed to suit the mounting arrangement for the tool it will be used on.

the work against the blade and then adjusting the pivot (Fig. 10-4). The problems with this method is that the blade must make four entry cuts and that at each one you must be careful to avoid bending the blade. Chances are that there will be rough spots at each entry point.

A better way to work is shown in Fig. 10-5. Use a piece of stock that is slightly oversize and make a freehand entry cut; then establish the pivot. You will waste some

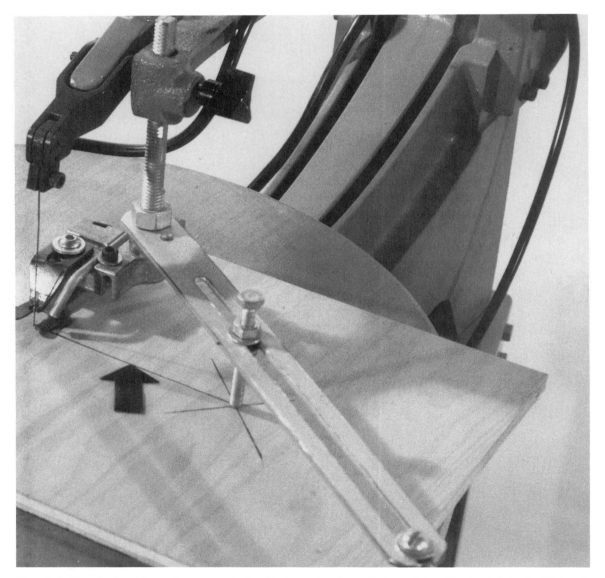

*Fig. 10-3.* The pivot point must be square to the blade and on line with the points of the blade's teeth. If this rule is not followed, the blade will not cut a true circle.

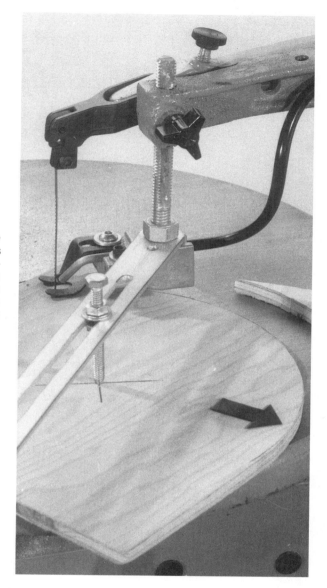

*Fig. 10-4.* Sawing can be done on square stock with dimensions that suit the diameter of the circle. The blade will have to make four entry cuts and this usually results in four rough places on the circumference. Arrow points to where this cut was started.

wood, but the cut will be continuous, which always contributes to accuracy and smoother edges all around.

Pivot sawing also can be done simply by providing an auxiliary platform that uses a nail as a pivot and that is held to the table with double-face tape or, when work size permits, with clamps (Fig. 10-6). The platform can be made for a single circle diameter—or for many—simply by supplying additional holes for the nail. You can drill a minimum-size hole for the blade or design the platform with an entry kerf as shown by the examples in Fig. 10-7.

The pivot-sawing technique can be used for more than full circles. Arc-shaped pieces, uniform or not, are among other possibilities. Ideas for this particular application are supplied by Figs. 10-8 through 10-10.

## SAWING ROUNDS: V-BLOCK WORK

Dowels and larger rounds can be cut efficiently on a scroll saw, but you must counter the blade's tendency to rotate the work. A firm grip as you saw is one

*Fig. 10-5.* A better procedure is to start with an oversize piece so the cut can be continuous. The job is started with a freehand cut to the line (arrow) before the pivot point is situated.

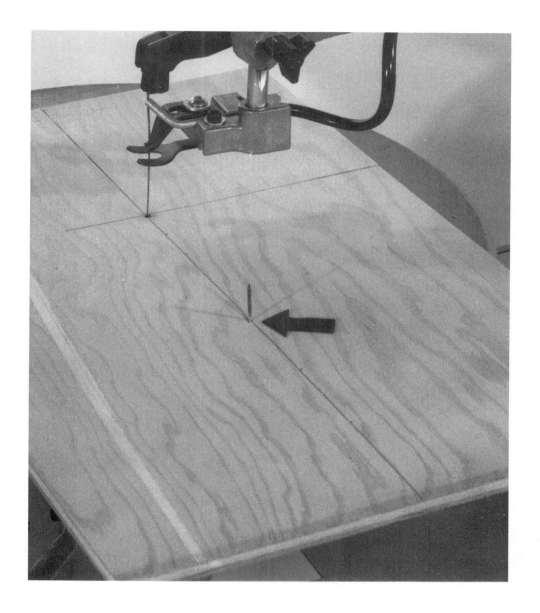

*Fig. 10-6.* An auxiliary platform with a nail through it that serves as a pivot is a simple way to organize for guided circular cuts. In this case, the blade is threaded through a hole that is drilled in the platform.

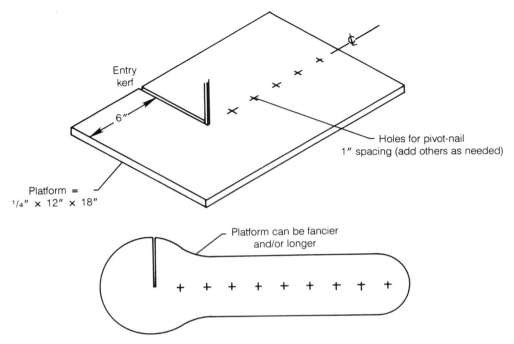

Entry
kerf

6″

Holes for pivot-nail
1″ spacing (add others as needed)

Platform =
¹/₄″ × 12″ × 18″

Platform can be fancier
and/or longer

+ + + + + + + + +

*Fig. 10-7.* Platform jigs can be organized for various circle sizes by providing a series of holes on a common centerline. An entry kerf made by the blade in use can be used in place of a blade insertion hole.

*Fig. 10-8.* You can form uniform arc-shaped pieces by sawing a rectangular piece of stock. The spacing of the pivot points determines the cross-sectional width of the arcs.

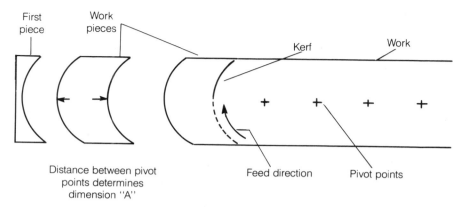

Fig. 10-9. When the pivot points are on a common centerline that is in line with the blade, the arcs will be uniform. The line for the pivots is the center of the workpiece.

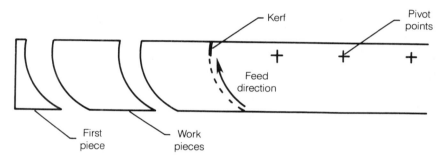

Fig. 10-10. Variations are possible by establishing pivot points on a line that is off the center of the work. The points still must be square to and on line with the blade.

answer, but a better solution, and one that will ensure square edges on the work-pieces, is to provide a V-block jig that will nestle the round stock so keeping it firm becomes a simple matter (Fig. 10-11). The jig must be kept square to the blade as it is moved. You can be sure of this by clamping a length of wood to the table that will serve as a fence against which the jig can ride.

When you need to produce multiple rounds of similar length, tap a nail into the center of the V and use it as a stop for the work (Fig. 10-12). The jig is drawn back after each cut and the round is moved to abut the nail so it will be positioned for the next cut.

The design for a V-block jig is provided in Fig. 10-13. It's easy to form the V if a table saw is handy. If not, form 45-degree chamfers on the edges of two pieces and then join them edge-to-edge.

The jig is a nice accessory to use whenever you need to saw through metal tubing or angles (Figs. 10-14 and 10-15). Use a metal piercing (jewelers) blade when sawing materials of this nature.

There are some phases of woodworking where it is necessary to join rounds in a particular fashion. Folks who make models that might involve dowel structures of one form or another find it necessary to use sawing techniques that ensure smooth, strong connections. Actually, these are joinery procedures but included here because we are talking about round workpieces.

When one dowel must cross or extend from another one, it must be shaped at its end or at some midpoint to match the circumference of the part it will be attached to. It will be difficult, if even possible, to be precise by controlling the work freehand-edly. Providing a holder that will keep the work secure—and also act as a guide for the cut—will ensure accuracy. The holder is a piece of suitably sized wood that has been drilled for the dowel and that has been sawed to the shape that is needed (Fig. 10-16). With the workpiece in place, sawing is done by following the cut path that is

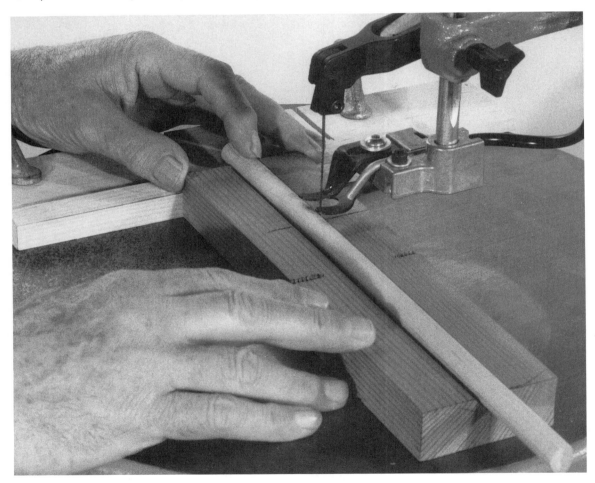

*Fig. 10-11.* The best way to saw dowels and other round stock is with a V-block jig. The clamped "fence" keeps the jig square to the blade.

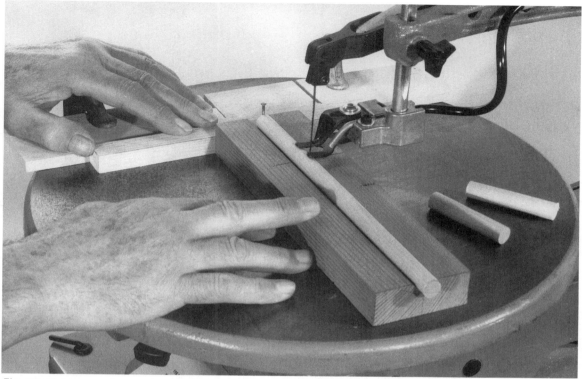

*Fig. 10-12.* Use a nail as a stop when you need to produce dowels of similar length. Note that the tool's hold-down is in place to help keep the work from rotating or moving up and down with the blade.

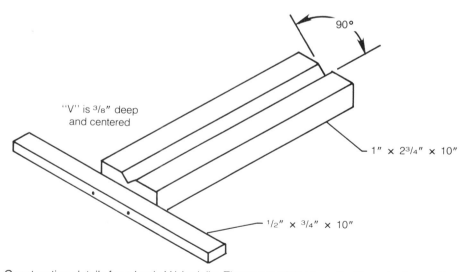

90°

''V'' is ³/₈'' deep and centered

1'' × 2³/₄'' × 10''

¹/₂'' × ³/₄'' × 10''

*Fig. 10-13.* Construction details for a basic V-block jig. The text explains how the V can be formed by sawing twin chamfers on separate pieces and then joining them.

*Fig. 10-14.* Cuts through metal tubing will be easy to do and accurate if you work with a V-block jig. Let the blade cut at its own pace—don't force.

in the holder. Careful sawing is required to prevent the blade from cutting into the fixture or moving away from it.

The same system is used for partial arcs like those needed for cope-type joints (Fig. 10-17). Figure 10-18 demonstrates how a simple work holder can be used when a round must be slotted. When possible, it's a good idea to first drill simultaneously through work and holder. When the diameter of the hole matches the width of the slot, two straight cuts complete the job.

## UNUSUAL BLADE APPLICATIONS

Some scroll saws offer the option of mounting blades so cutting can be done at right angles to the arm of the machine. This allows rip-type cuts on oversize workpieces. With scroll saws without this option, you can still utilize the idea simply by twisting both ends of the blade 90 degrees (Fig. 10-19). Tempering is not typical at blade ends so it is possible to alter them without fear of breakage. This is done with pliers— one gripping the blade where the teeth end, and the other on the blank portion. It is

*Fig. 10-15.* Angles are another form that is easier to saw when supported in a V. Use a metal piercing (jewelers) blade when sawing metals.

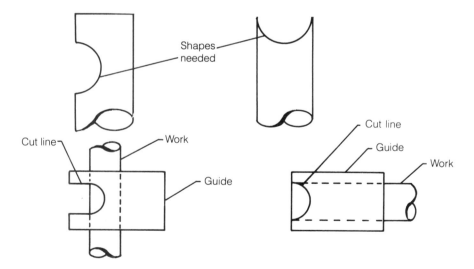

*Fig. 10-16.* Accurate shapes can be formed on the ends or at some midpoint on round stock when a holder is used. The holder does two jobs—it keeps the work secure and serves as a pattern for the cut.

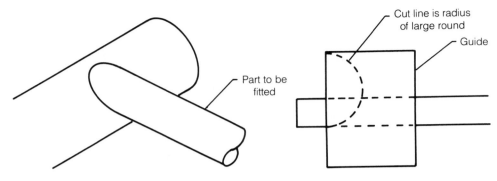

*Fig. 10-17.* Using a holder to form a cope cut.

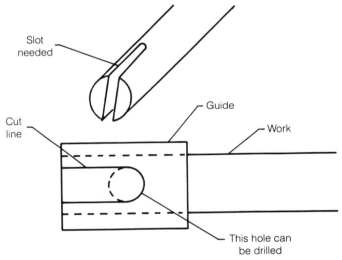

*Fig. 10-18.* A special holder allows sawing slots in the end of cylinders. Two straight cuts complete the job if a hole is drilled first. The diameter of the hole matches the width of the slot.

not the perfect solution because blade action on some scroll saws involves a slight rocking motion, but it's worth a try even though sawing results might be less than perfect.

Do you need a kerf that is wider than the heaviest blade you have will provide? You can do the job by making parallel, overlapping cuts, or twin cuts between which the waste material is removed. You also could try the idea that is shown in Fig. 10-20, where several blades are assembled and mounted so they will cut as one. You might be able to grip all blades in top and bottom clamps or chucks, depending on the machine. If not, you can still use the idea by cutting off the blank end of extra blades and securing them to a single blade that can be mounted in regular fashion.

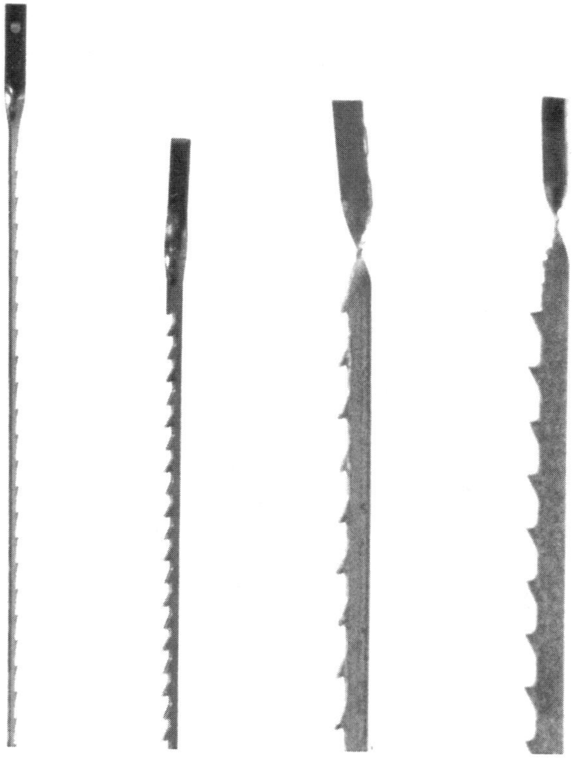

*Fig. 10-19.* Twisting the ends of scrollsaw-blades is an easy task. When modified this way they can be installed for sawing at right angles to the arm of the machine. It's a nice idea to use when the blade clamps on a machine allow only a normal blade position.

Blades can be held together with short lengths of strong, thin wire or you can make a permanent assembly by bonding the blades with a type of magic glue. Slot-type cuts that are possible by using the blade-assembly idea are useful for slip joints and for the cuts that are required for the egg crate assembly that will be shown later in this chapter. The technique does not provide complete freedom. It's not reasonable to expect to make cuts that are 1/2 inch wide, but you will do well if you stay in the area of slot widths that are 1/4 inch or less. The thought assumes the use of blades that are reasonably wide. There are greater limitations if the blade assemblies are composed of fine blades.

If you or a fellow woodworker owns a band saw, you can have a supply of heavy-duty scroll saw blades by making use of loop-type blades that have been discarded for use on the parent machine. What you must do is cut the discarded blade to suitable lengths for the scroll saw and then grind the ends to form blanks that will fit the tool's clamps or chucks (Fig. 10-21). These improvised blades will not make super-smooth cuts, but they are quite suitable for sawing thick stock (Fig. 10-22).

Band saw blades will break easily if you use flat-nose pliers at the break point and a second pair of pliers to flex the blade until it snaps. The break won't be clean but a little touching up with a file or on a grinder will make it right.

Hacksaw blades, that you can use for sawing metals, can be recycled the same

*Fig. 10-20.* Ganging blades allows making cuts that are much wider than a normal kerf. The idea works best with fairly wide blades.

way, but you must be more careful when breaking them to length. The best way is to grip them at the break point in the jaws of a vise and then, after covering them with a cloth, rap them sharply with a hammer. As always, when doing any shopwork, show your safety wisdom by wearing eye protection.

## SANDING

Any scroll saw that has clamp or chuck-type arrangements to secure blades can be organized to do a degree of light-duty sanding. The idea is to supply a strip of abrasive material that can be gripped between upper and lower arms as if it was a saw

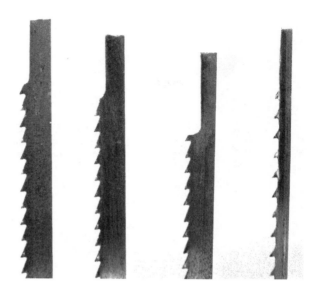

*Fig. 10-21.* You can make your own scroll-saw blades by salvaging used band-saw and hacksaw blades. Ends must be ground or filed to a width that allows installation in the tool's blade clamps.

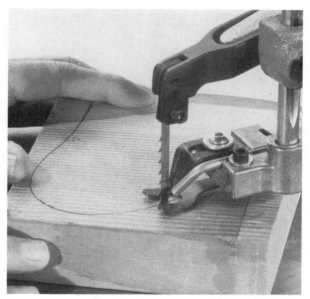

*Fig. 10-22.* Homemade blades, because they can be wider than commercial products, can often make it easier to saw through thick material.

blade. One way to go is to cut to length, and modify the ends of emery boards—those "sticks" used to smooth fingernails—so they will serve the purpose (Fig. 10-23). The emery boards, for this use, are rather flexible. Supply a slip of wood as a backup that can be positioned as shown in Fig. 10-24 so you can bear more heavily against the abrasive surface.

Fig. 10-23. Emery boards, normally used for smoothing fingernails, can be modified and mounted like saw blades for light sanding jobs.

Fig. 10-24. Emery boards are fairly flexible but, when necessary, you can use a strip of wood as a backup.

A substitute arrangement can be provided by shaping a strip of aluminum—or some similar material—so it can be correctly mounted in the machine and then covering its working area with self-adhesive sandpaper (Fig. 10-25). There is an advantage with this method—self-adhesive sandpaper is available in more grit sizes than you will find on conventional emery boards.

Fixed-arm machines that have a lower chuck to grip blades have an advantage when it comes to sanding. Because the chucks can grip round shanks, small-size drum sanders can be used very efficiently (Fig. 10-26). Some manufacturers, like Delta, offer sanding accessories like the unit that is shown in Fig. 10-27 that has a half-round and a flat surface. Thus it can be used to smooth arcs or straight edges. Figures 10-28 and 10-29 offer suggestions for homemade sanding accessories. Often, a sanding chore will be easier to do if a sander is custom designed for the purpose. Most times, when a tool allows the type of drum sanding we have been discussing, it will be necessary to work without the table's insert. It won't be a bother when workpieces are large, but to supply support when small components are involved, it will be necessary to custom make substitute inserts (Fig. 10-30).

*Fig. 10-25.* Another way to provide sanding sticks for the saw is to shape a strip of thin metal so it can be gripped by the blade clamps and then covering its working area with self-adhesive sandpaper.

*Fig. 10-26 (left).* Small drum sanders can be used if the machine's lower blade holder can grip round-shank tools. This pretty much limits their use to fixed-arm concepts.

*Fig. 10-27 (above).* Commercial drum sanders, like this one offered by Delta, are available. It has a half-round shape so it can be used to smooth concave shapes and straight edges.

## FILING

Machine files can be used on scroll saws that have lower chucks to grip blades (Fig. 10-31). This pretty much limits their use to fixed-arm machines. The files are available in various shapes—round, half-round, triangular—so they can be used to smooth edges on the interior or exterior of almost any pattern whether lines are curved or straight (Fig. 10-32).

Run the machine at a slow speed and feed the work gently against the file. Keep the workpiece moving. If you hesitate, the file will indent edges. It's okay to use machine files to smooth edges of wood, but you must use a very light feed pressure and clean the files frequently. Soft materials can quickly become impacted between cutting points or abrasive particles so that the tool will do more rubbing than filing.

## SAWING MATERIALS OTHER THAN WOOD

The scroll saw can be used to cut many nonwood materials ranging from ferrous metals and ceramic tile through paper. Each of the materials must be handled in a

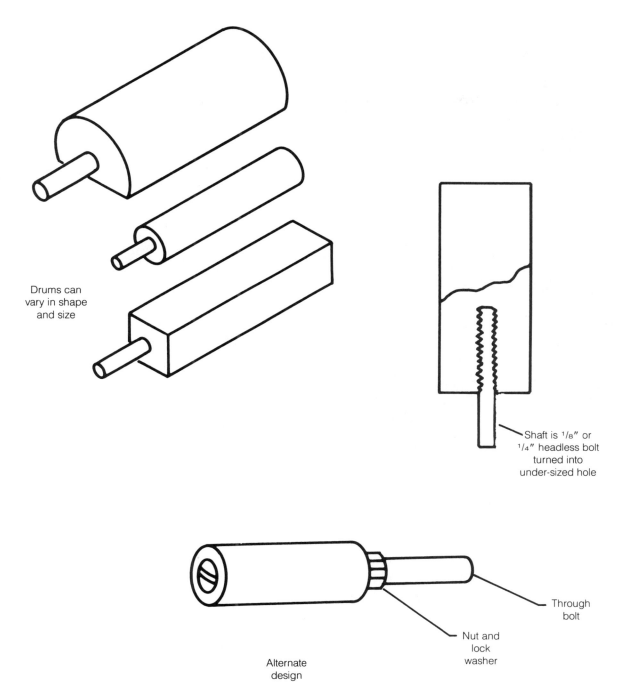

Drums can
vary in shape
and size

Shaft is 1/8" or
1/4" headless bolt
turned into
under-sized hole

Through
bolt

Nut and
lock
washer

Alternate
design

*Fig. 10-28.* You can make drum sanders by following these ideas. Provide the abrasive by using self-adhesive sandpaper.

**Fig. 10-29.** It's okay to work without the tool's insert when sanding large pieces.

particular way for success. Different blades and speeds, how the work is prepared, its thickness, even the machine in use has a bearing on the best way to go. An entire chapter could be devoted to each of the products, but the book would end up a thousand pages thick. Even then, some information would be lacking because of the many variables to be considered.

In the final analysis, good practice calls for some experimentation with blades, feeds, and speeds when you need to saw an alien material. There are some basic considerations, and it's possible that the owner's manual might supply some specifies to lead you in the right direction.

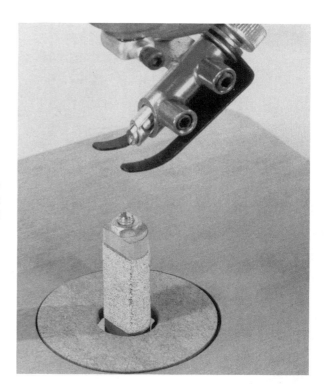

*Fig. 10-30.* When parts are very small, you must supply support close to the sander by providing a special insert.

## SAWING METALS

Metals can be "hard" or "soft." Although some metals can be cut with regular blades, it's best to use metal piercing (jewelers) blades for all applications. Soft metals, such as brass and some types of aluminum cut easily, but steel and iron take a little more doing. Often, hard metals will saw more easily if the blade is lubricated or rubbed with a cake of paraffin (Fig. 10-33) or a wax candle. Even a touch of hard, paste wax on the blade can help make sawing easier and extend blade life.

Soft metals of reasonable thickness can be sawed with blades that have many teeth, as many as 36 TPI, and at a fairly fast CS/M. Hard metals, especially as they increase in thickness, should be sawed with coarser blades, at reduced speeds, and with careful feed pressure. Cutting will go slowly; trying to go faster than the blade can cut will only result in poor work and premature blade dulling and breakage.

Thin sheet metals tend to bend down or burr out along the bottom of the kerf. To prevent this from happening or, at least, to minimize it, attach an auxiliary platform to the table with clamps or double-face tape. The platform should be drilled so there will be zero clearance around the blade. The platform that was suggested for pivot sawing earlier in this chapter might serve nicely (Fig. 10-34). Another way to avoid the nuisance of bends and burrs is to saw with the workpiece sandwiched between pieces of plywood or hardboard (Fig. 10-35).

*Fig. 10-31.* The comment made about drum sanders also applies to machine files. They can be used only if the machine is equipped with a lower chuck.

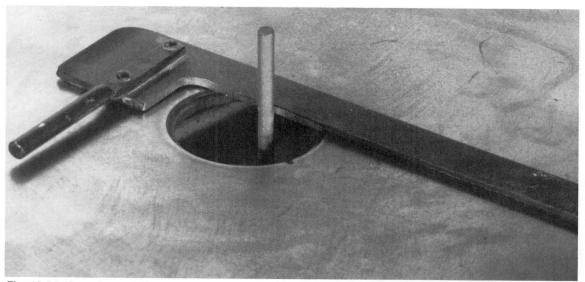

*Fig. 10-32.* Keep the workpiece moving when using files and use a very light feed pressure. Files of this type will gum up very quickly if you use them to smooth wood.

*Fig. 10-33.* Metals can be sawed more easily and blades will last longer if you occasionally place a drop of lubricant on the cut line. (Dremel photo.)

## SAWING PLASTICS

A major consideration when sawing plastics is to do whatever is possible to minimize heat buildup around the cutting area. When the blade heats up, as it must because of the friction it generates while working, it can cause some types of plastic to soften enough to fuse in the kerf—even to the point of binding the blade. This might not be a problem on dense plastics such as Corian (Fig. 10-36), which cuts about as cleanly as hardwood, but it is not unusual on products such as Lucite and Plexiglas.

A thought here before I go further, is to imagine a fused kerf as a design element. A little farfetched perhaps, but it is a fun application that can provide some novel effects (Fig. 10-37). The fused lines might not be solid, but they will be obvious.

Generally, it is good practice to provide as much clearance in the kerf by using blades with teeth that have maximum set. Using coarse blades is helpful, but large teeth can cause chipping where the blade comes through on the underside of the workpiece. Try slight blades and a slow speed to begin with. Make changes in both areas as you feel they are necessary. Very thin plastics can be handled as if they were sheet metal. That is, provide an auxiliary platform or sandwich the material between pieces of plywood or hardboard.

Most plastics come with paper covers that should be kept in place while sawing. The covers protect the plastic, provide a convenient way to mark patterns, and help to some extent to keep the blade running cooler (Figs. 10-38 and 10-39).

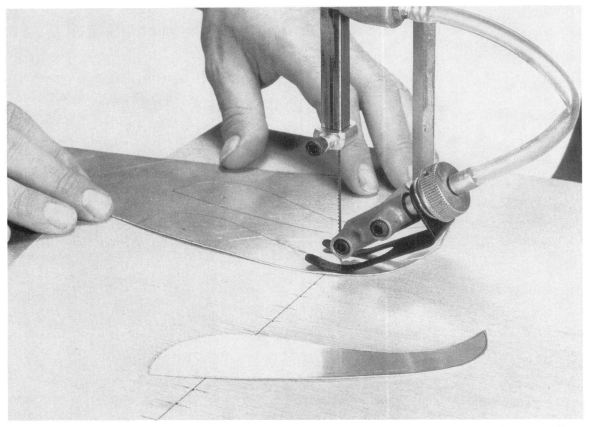

*Fig. 10-34.* You can practically eliminate bending and burring when sawing thin sheets by using an auxiliary platform that is drilled for zero clearance around the blade. This platform is the same one that was used for pivot sawing.

*Fig. 10-35.* An even more effective way to eliminate bending and burring is to sandwich the work between sheets of plywood or hardboard.

An idea that works toward cooler cutting whether the plastic has protective covers or not, is to supply lubrication on the pattern line by rubbing over it with a block of paraffin or even a wax crayon (Fig. 10-40).

## SAWING PAPER

Many scroll saw craftspeople will use the pad-sawing method to produce multiple, similar designs that can be used for, among other things, Christmas and greeting cards. Good results are guaranteed, provided the sheets of paper are tightly sandwiched between layers of plywood or some other material such as hardboard or

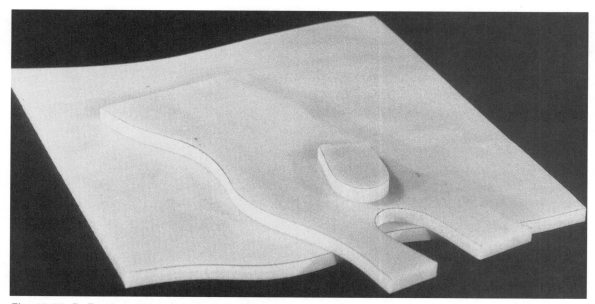

*Fig. 10-36.* DuPont's methacrylate Corian saws like a dense hardwood. Fine jewelers blades can be used to produce smooth edges. The material does not weld in the kerf.

*Fig. 10-37.* Sawing should be done to avoid welded kerfs, but you can produce interesting design elements if you deliberately allow it to happen.

*Fig. 10-38.* Keep the paper covers on the plastic until sawing is complete. The paper protects the plastic and provides a means of marking patterns.

*Fig. 10-39.* The paper covers help to keep the blade running cooler. Adjust the nozzle of the blower so air will be directed toward the blade just above the surface of the stock.

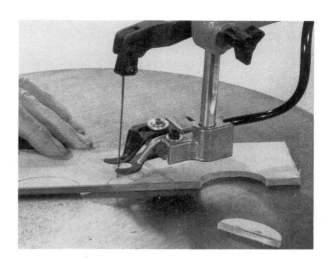

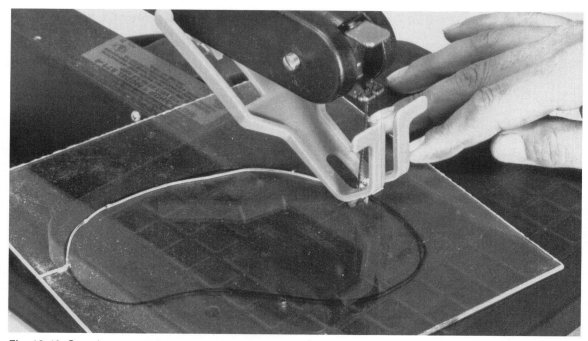

*Fig. 10-40.* Covering pattern lines with paraffin or a wax crayon also helps to keep blade and material cooler. Try this whether or not the plastic has paper covers. (Dremel photo.)

heavy posterboard (Fig. 10-41). The paper and the covers should be large enough so that the nails that are used to hold the pad together can penetrate through an area that will not mar the pattern. Paper that is sawed by using the pad method will have remarkably smooth edges (Fig. 10-42).

## SAMPLING OF OTHER MATERIALS

Materials such as vinyl or cork floor tiles can be easily sawed on the scroll saw (Fig. 10-43). If the cuts are simple, straight ones, you might just as well work with a knife and straightedge as you would normally. For cutouts that are required to place a tile around a pipe or similar obstruction, using the scroll saw will make the job easier to do more accurately. You can work with conventional blades, but use a slow CS/M and a cautious feed to ensure that the blade will stay on the pattern line.

You are not about to saw ceramic tiles with regular saw blades, but if the machine allows the use of saber saw-type blades, you can do such work with the "grit-edge" blades that are offered by Remington. The blades don't "saw," but abrade with hundreds of particles of tungsten carbide (Fig. 10-44). Getting through tough, brittle material is no problem, but you must work carefully. Use a slow speed and don't force the cut. Keep the workpiece firmly down on the table to avoid vibration; use the tool's hold-down when you can. Blade widths negate intricate cutting but generous curves are possible. Sawing is on the slow side, so work patiently.

# JOINERY ON THE SCROLL SAW

Let's start off by being honest. If your shop equipment includes a table or radial arm saw and a portable router that is supported by a complement of jigs and fixtures, you might not be inclined to use a scroll saw to shape joints. On the other hand, if a scroll saw is the main shop tool, then plan to utilize its capabilities in joinery areas. Regardless of how extensive your equipment is, there is nothing wrong with discovering

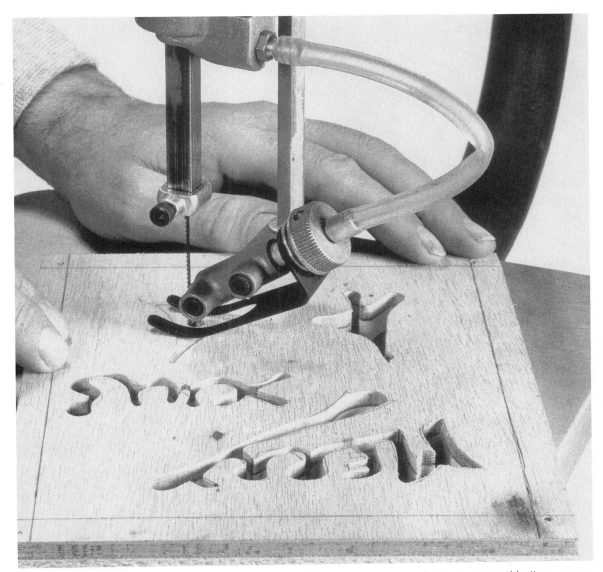

*Fig. 10-41.* You can saw quantities of paper by sandwiching a pad of sheets between top and bottom covers. The paper must be gripped tightly.

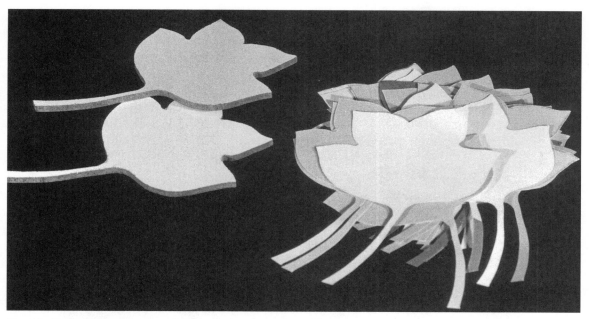

Fig. 10-42. Pad-sawed paper will have feather-free edges. The heavy pieces at the left were the covers for the pad.

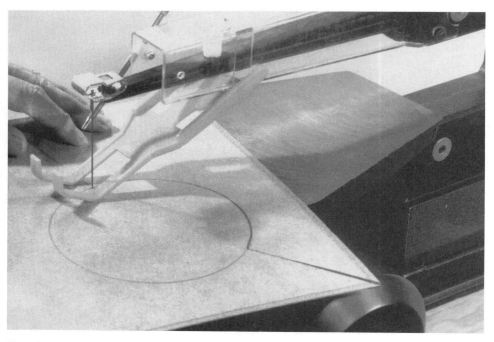

Fig. 10-43. Vinyl floor tile saws very easily. Cutouts needed to place tiles around obstructions can be done very accurately.

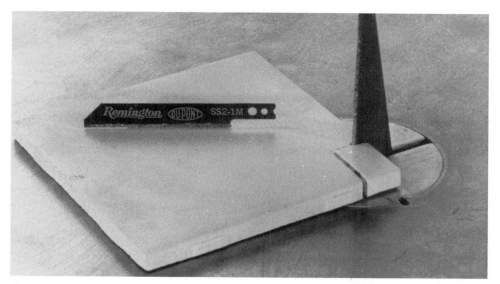

*Fig. 10-44.* Remington's "grit-edge" blades can be used to saw ceramic tile, so long as the machine can accommodate blades that are meant to be used in portable saber saws.

how the scroll saw can be used in this area of woodworking. Another thought is that innovations can lead to unique connections that might not be possible on other tools. Also, the scroll saw will allow some custom interpretations of standard joints. A case in point is the dovetail joint. Most standard dovetail-joint fixtures that are designed for use with a portable router, dictate the size and the spacing of the pins and tails. If you do the work on a scroll saw, you can decide the number of connections and the spacing between them. More about dovetails a bit later.

In general, success in making acceptable joints on the scroll saw depends on how carefully you work. Accuracy is paramount when you are cutting two pieces that must mesh as one. It's a little different than, for example, sawing a profile plaque where some slight variations from the pattern will not be serious.

## END LAP JOINTS

End lap joints are used to join pieces end-to-end or so that they turn a corner. The parts can be of similar or dissimilar widths, but of equal thickness. When parts are joined, surfaces will be flush (Fig. 10-45). Cutting is done with the material on edge so stock widths that can be cut will be limited by the capacity of the machine. Work with a wide blade that is tensioned enough to avoid bowing in the cut, and be sure the angle between blade and table is 90 degrees. Careful sawing will produce good results, but if the sawed surfaces are rougher than you like because of the blade that is used, you can saw a fraction outside the layout lines and then do some sanding by hand to finish up. Sandpaper wrapped tightly around a wooden block makes a good tool for the final work.

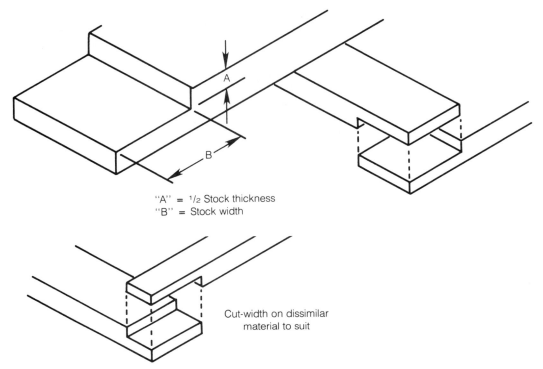

"A" = ½ Stock thickness
"B" = Stock width

Cut-width on dissimilar
material to suit

*Fig. 10-45.* End lap joints can be formed on material of equal or dissimilar widths.

## CROSS LAPS

Cross laps, detailed in Fig. 10-46, require forming slots to suit the thicknesses of mating pieces. The work can be done entirely on the saw, but it will be easier to make parallel shoulder cuts to the depth that is required and then remove the waste by working with a sharp chisel.

Eggcrate assemblies (Fig. 10-47) require the same kind of sawing, but usually, the thickness of the components allows the use of the pad-sawing method. Think about grouping several blades to form a wide slot. The job will be much easier if you can saw a "kerf" that matches the thickness of the parts. Cut depth equals one half the stock's width.

## FINGERLAPS

The appeal of the fingerlap joint lies in its appearance and its structural strength, which is because of the great amount of gluing surfaces afforded by the interlocking fingers. To do the multiple fingerlap on the scroll saw would be quite a chore. If you reduce its design to a single connection, it becomes reasonable to do and will have practical uses (Fig. 10-48). The length of the finger is arbitrary; the depth of the cut in the mating piece suits the thickness of the stock.

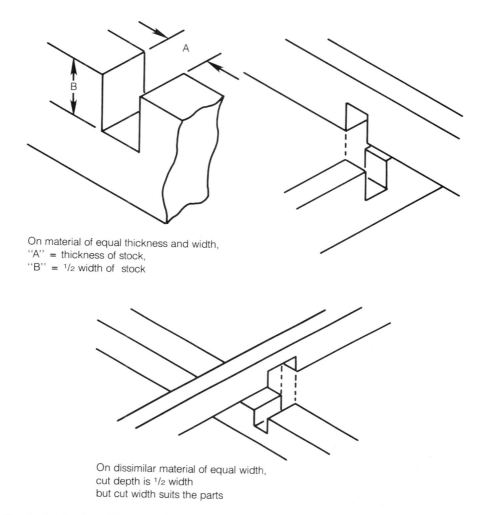

On material of equal thickness and width,
"A" = thickness of stock,
"B" = 1/2 width of stock

On dissimilar material of equal width,
cut depth is 1/2 width
but cut width suits the parts

*Fig. 10-46.* Basics of the cross lap joint.

To supply additional strength and a locking feature so the joint won't come apart should the glue fail, it's a simple matter to drill a hole through the parts after assembly and insert a dowel (Fig. 10-49). Adding a dowel leads to other ideas. If the dowel fits tightly in one part, but loosely in the other, you have a swivel joint (Fig. 10-50). The amount of movement will depend on the amount of work you do after the parts of the joint have been formed. If you modify to the extent shown in Fig. 10-51, the parts can swing in arcs greater than 180 degrees.

Applications? Well, just for starters, think of toy projects like the swiveling crocodile shown in Fig. 10-52.

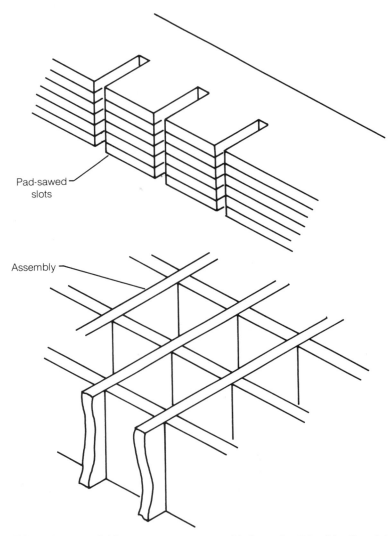

Pad-sawed slots

Assembly

*Fig. 10-47.* When the material for an eggcrate assembly is on the thin side, the slots can be formed by pad sawing. Slot depth is one half the materials width. Slot width equals the materials thickness.

## DOVETAIL JOINTS

The dovetail joint, like the fingerlap, is one of the classic wood connections. When done with multiple pins and tails, as the parts are called (Fig. 10-53), there is considerable gluing area, but the outstanding feature of the joint is the way mating forms interlock. The joint will stay together even if the glue should fail.

Doing multiple dovetails on the scroll saw can be a trying chore, one calling for patience and absolute accuracy. My personal feeling is that if a portable router and special dovetail jigs are available, the work is done best on that type of equipment. Some jigs dictate uniform spacing of pins and tails, but there are others that allow some custom designing along the lines of number of dovetails and their placement. It's not my intention to discourage—merely to make a point. Perfectly good dovetailing can be accomplished on the scroll saw and, a point in its favor, no special accessories are required.

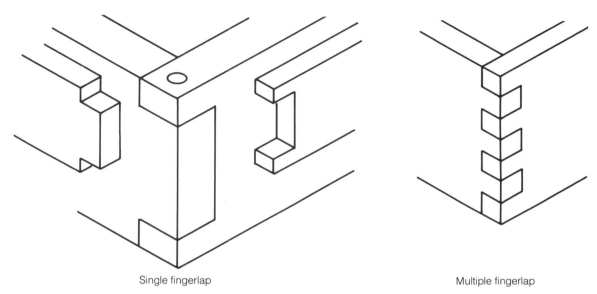

Single fingerlap                                                                                    Multiple fingerlap

*Fig. 10-48.* The single fingerlap is a reasonable job for a scroll saw. The multiple design is, of course, also feasible. It just requires more time and patience.

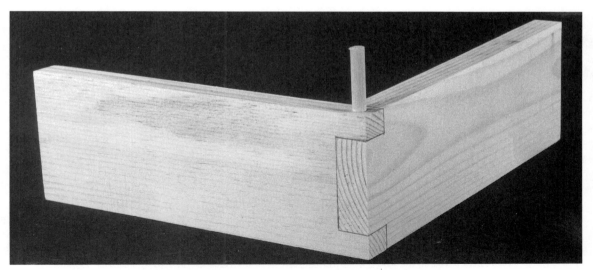

*Fig. 10-49.* Inserting a dowel after the joint is assembled provides a locking feature.

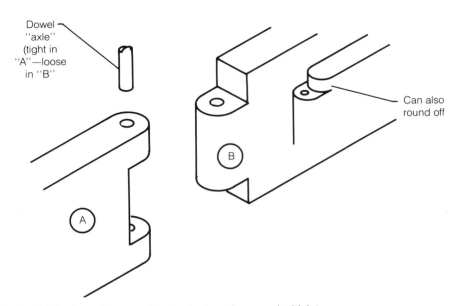

*Fig. 10-50.* The fingerlap can also be designed as a swivel joint.

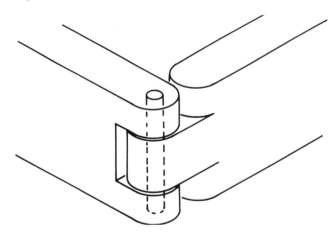

*Fig. 10-51.* The extent of the swivel action is determined by how the parts of the joint are modified.

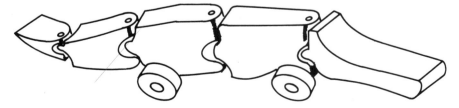

*Fig. 10-52.* The swivel joint makes it possible to produce, among other things, toys like this jointed crocodile.

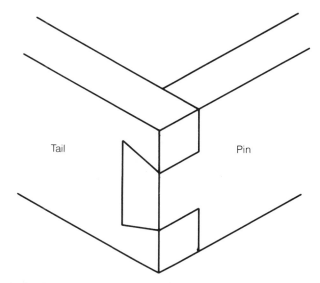

**Fig. 10-53.** The single dovetail joint is a good way to become acquainted with the saw cuts that are needed to produce the joint.

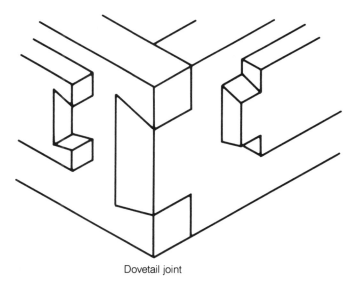

Dovetail joint

**Fig. 10-54.** Mating parts of the dovetail joint.

The best way to learn the procedure is to produce a single dovetail on some reasonably good stock (Figs. 10-54 through 10-56). Select pieces that are the same width and be sure they have square ends. Start by forming the pin because it requires more attention that the tail and can be used like a pattern to mark how the tail should be cut.

Mark a line parallel to the end of the stock and spaced to equal the stock's thickness. Lay out perpendicular lines to indicate the length of the pin and from the end of these lines draw angular lines of 15 degrees across the stock's edge.

The first saw cut is made with the machine's table tilted 15 degrees as shown in Fig. 10-57. The second cut, because it slants in a different direction, must be made

*Fig. 10-55.* Very careful sawing is required for the parts of the dovetail joint to mesh as they should.

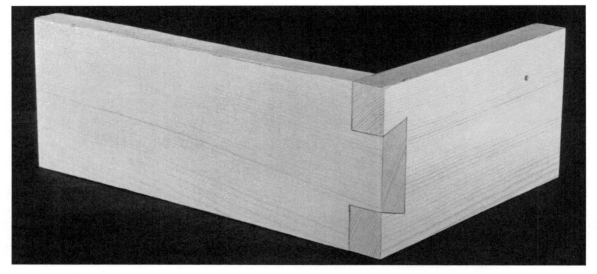

*Fig. 10-56.* The dovetail joint is often left exposed as a mark of craftsmanship. The joint is attractive and has a locking feature that will keep parts together even if the glue fails.

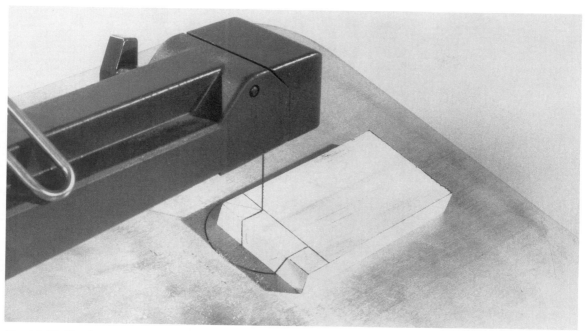

*Fig. 10-57.* The first step is to make the angular cuts for the pin. The cuts slant in different directions so the second cut must be made with the table tilted in the opposite direction. The text offers a suggestion for doing the job if the table can be tilted in only one direction.

after the table has been tilted 15 degrees from horizontal in the opposite direction. There is a trick you can use if the table can't be tilted in two directions. Leave the table in its original setting but mount the blade backward. Then, with the work on the rear of the table, pull the work toward you to make the second angular cut.

The next step is done with the table in horizontal position. Make straight cuts to the angular ones as shown in Fig. 10-58. This will remove the bulk of the waste, but a triangular section (indicated by the arrow in the photograph) will have to be removed by hand with a chisel or a sharp knife. Another trick you can try if the machine allows it, is mount the blade 90 degrees from its normal position and make the cuts with the table still tilted as shown in Fig. 10-59. With this method the entire waste piece is removed.

Use the finished pin as a pattern to mark the second piece. Place it very carefully and trace around it with a sharp, hard pencil. Saw cuts that are required for the tail are all straight and done with the table in horizontal position (Fig. 10-60).

## END-TO-END JOINTS

The type of joints that are shown in Figs. 10-61 and 10-62 are handy when you wish to join small panels or boards. There are two ways to do them. Make the cut in one

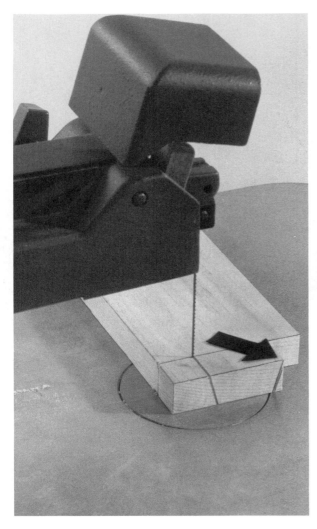

*Fig. 10-58.* The cut to remove the waste is made, usually, with the table in horizontal position. This will leave a triangular piece (arrow) that must be removed by hand with a chisel or knife—or you can use a coping saw.

part and use it as a pattern to mark the second piece, or, overlap the ends that will be joined and make the cut simultaneously in both pieces. The latter idea does waste a little wood but the job goes more quickly and with the assurance that the parts will fit precisely. No particular pattern is required. In fact, it's kind of fun to do the sawing in a haphazard way so long as you provide for an interlocking feature.

## COPE JOINTS

Cope joints are often used when similar moldings must meet at an inside corner. This type of connection is preferred by many carpenters because the joint is less likely to show the gap that can happen when wood shrinkage can cause a conventional miter joint to separate.

*Fig. 10-59.* If the blade can be mounted 90 degrees from its normal position, the entire waste piece can be sawed off by working with the table in the original tilt position. If necessary, this is a good place to make use of the twisted blade end idea.

The system calls for using one piece as is, butting it into the corner, but cutting the second one to the profile shape of the molding (Fig. 10-63). You might be able to scribe the outline of the cut, but there is a simpler way to do it. Make a 45-degree miter on the second piece and then do the coping by using the outside edge of the miter as a pattern. The pieces will butt together but the appearance will be that of a conventional miter joint (Fig. 10-64). Figure 10-65 shows how to do the work when the molding is something like quarter round.

*Fig. 10-60.* The finished pin is used as a pattern to mark the mating piece. The sawing is done with the table in horizontal position. All cuts are straight.

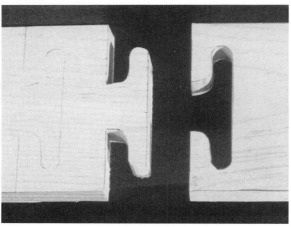

*Fig. 10-61.* Use the scroll saw to shape interlocking end-to-end joints. The shapes to use are arbitrary.

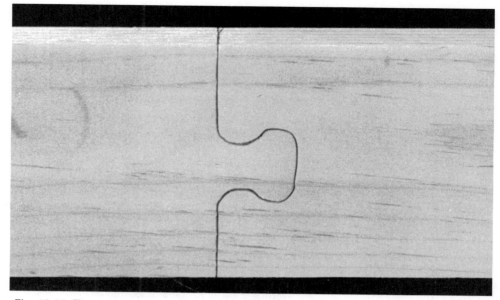

*Fig. 10-62.* The parts can be sawed individually, or simultaneously if you overlap the ends of the components. Using the overlap method will waste some wood but will reduce sawing time and ensure accuracy.

One way to do a coped joint

One piece is cut to match the profile of the mating piece.

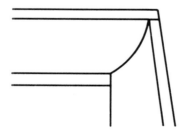

After assembly, the appearance is that of a miter joint.

*Fig. 10-63.* The parts of a cope joint butt together but the appearance is that of a miter joint.

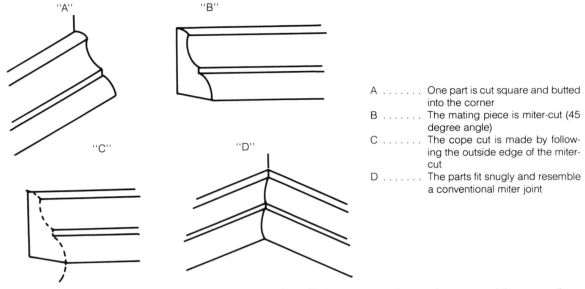

"A"    "B"

"C"    "D"

A . . . . . . .  One part is cut square and butted
               into the corner
B . . . . . . .  The mating piece is miter-cut (45
               degree angle)
C . . . . . . .  The cope cut is made by follow-
               ing the outside edge of the miter-
               cut
D . . . . . . .  The parts fit snugly and resemble
               a conventional miter joint

*Fig. 10-64.* The steps that are needed to form a cope joint. These steps can be used on any molding regardless of its profile.

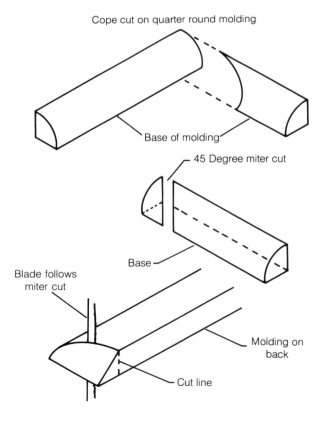

Cope cut on quarter round molding

Base of molding

45 Degree miter cut

Base

Blade follows
miter cut

Molding on
back

Cut line

*Fig. 10-65.* This is how the cope joint is formed for material such as quarter-round molding.

# Chapter 11

# Patterns and Layout

THE FIRST STEP IN SCROLL SAW WORK IS TO PROVIDE A PATTERN THAT YOU CAN "TRACE" with the saw blade. Even straight lines, whether you saw them freehand or by using a guide, should be marked so you will have an ongoing check of whether the job is being done accurately. Patterns can be original or you can copy them directly or with some modifications from available sources—and there are many sources. Aside from those that can be purchased full size, mostly from craftsman supply houses, there are newspapers, magazines, catalogs, calendars, books, greeting cards, and photographs. The decision to make is whether to save the original. If not, and assuming its size suits the project you have in mind, you can simply tear it from the periodical and attach it to the workpiece with a spray adhesive or rubber cement. If you wish to save the original (I assume you won't be tearing pages from the project section of this book!), there are other options.

## THE SQUARES METHOD

A traditional system for duplicating patterns while retaining the original is enlarging or reducing by using the squares method that is demonstrated in Figs. 11-1 and 11-2. It's simple and allows an exact, smaller, or larger reproduction whether or not you are an artist. Select a sheet of tracing paper that is larger than the illustration and mark it with squares. You can judge the size of the squares by the intricacy of the pattern. The more complex it is, the smaller the squares should be. Let's assume you start with 1/2-inch squares. Use some masking tape to hold the tracing paper over the pattern. Now, with paper that will be the actual pattern you will use to saw with, draw squares of equal or smaller or larger size than those on the tracing paper; it depends on the size you wish the project to be.

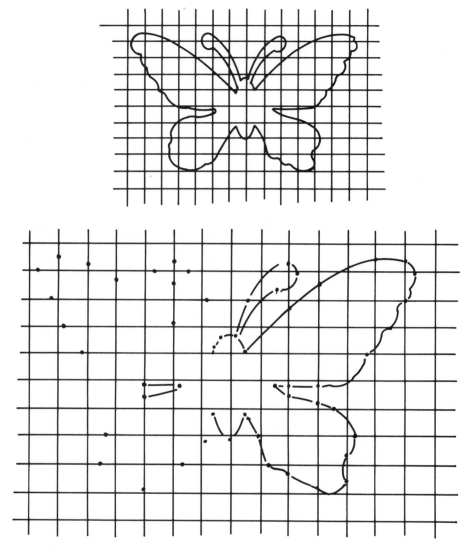

*Fig. 11-1.* Patterns can be duplicated in smaller or larger sizes by using the squares method. If, for example, the grid over the original has 1/4-inch squares, and the grid for the duplicate has 1/2-inch squares, the pattern will be double the size of the original illustration.

The next step is to mark crucial points that you can see through the tracing paper onto corresponding points on the pattern paper. Be generous with the number of points you mark, especially if the pattern is complex. The more marks, the easier it will be to connect them correctly. Then it's a question of drawing from mark to mark to expose the pattern. It's something like those dotted children's pictures where the pattern becomes real after the dots are connected.

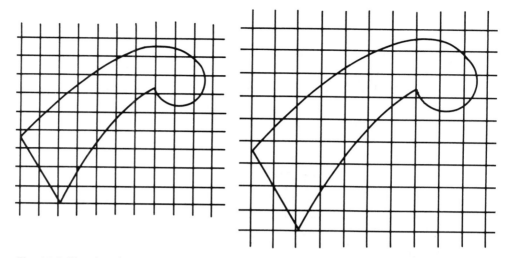

*Fig. 11-2.* The dots that are marked on the duplication grid can be connected freehand, but if curves are fairly uniform, work with something like a French curve to draw the outlines.

*Fig. 11-3.* If you choose to cut out patterns, work with a sharp knife and with the pattern taped to a hard material, such as a smooth-surfaced, tempered hardboard.

## ATTACHING PATTERNS TO THE WORKPIECE

Now you have to decide whether to sacrifice the pattern by attaching it to the work-piece or whether to save it. Saving it makes sense because you worked hard to pro-duce it and it might have future use. One way to go is to transfer the design to the workpiece by using carbon paper. Some workers will use a needle or a tracing wheel to puncture the pattern and cause indents that outline the pattern on the workpiece. It works, but it doesn't do the pattern much good and it isn't the easiest thing to do on hardwood. Also, you still have dots to connect when sawing.

## PATTERNS AS TEMPLATES

A better way is to cut out the pattern so it can be used as a template to mark the work (Figs. 11-3 and 11-4). This method does not violate the pattern and provides clean lines to follow when sawing. If this method is selected, draw the pattern, whether original or duplicated, on reasonably heavy paper or posterboard.

*Fig. 11-4.* Use a fairly heavy paper or some thin posterboard when patterns are cut out so they can be used as templates. The pencil needs a reasonable edge to be guided by.

## USING A COPYING MACHINE

I can think of few items that can be more helpful to a scroll saw user than a copying machine. Any illustration you can find or create can be duplicated on paper that can serve as a sawing pattern (Fig. 11-5). Copying machine establishments can be found most anywhere and the machines at their disposal will enlarge or reduce. When you can have more than one copy made, you can be nonchalant about attaching one directly to the workpiece even though it will be destroyed during sawing.

I feel that a copying machine is an asset to the scroll saw enthusiast. It's okay to work with a business place, but having one at your disposal makes things a lot easier, and offers innovative uses. For example, as shown in Figs. 11-6 and 11-7, you can use solid objects to provide sawing patterns. Look at the designs in Fig. 11-8; they are patterns of clock hands that were made on a copying machine. I guess that thinking of acquiring a copying machine as a scroll saw accessory comes down to

*Fig. 11-5.* Any illustration can be duplicated on a copying machine.

*Fig. 11-6.* The outline of solid objects can also be duplicated on a copier. This letter was shaped on a scroll saw.

cost, and a decision must be based on your involvement in scroll saw activity. It's one thing if your use is casual, another if you are completely enthralled or the tool serves a main purpose in a cottage industry. Anyway, whether you buy or rent or run down to a local store, don't overlook the help a copier can provide.

## TOOLS TO USE FOR LAYOUT WORK

The common combination square (Fig. 11-9), can be used as a ruler for straight lines, to mark lines at 90 degrees to an edge, or to check or lay out 45-degree angular cuts. A carpenter's square is usable on large workpieces for straight lines or checking square corners, and when utilized as shown in Figs. 11-10 and 11-11, for marking angular cuts. The idea comes in handy when laying out the cut angles for a segmented assembly.

You can duplicate an existing profile by using a pair of dividers or a compass as shown in Fig. 11-12. Hold the tool vertically and keep the point and the pencil on a line that is perpendicular to the pattern's contour.

Draftsman's templates, such as the French curve used in Fig. 11-13 can certainly be useful. All of the shapes and lines that are shown in Fig. 11-14 were drawn with a single French curve.

Circle templates (Fig. 11-15) make it easy to draw precise rounded corners. It's best to use the template first and then to draw the tangent lines to the arcs.

*Fig. 11-7.* An advantage of a copying machine is that the original illustration can be enlarged or reduced to suit how you envision the project.

Figure 11-16 suggests a way to construct a ''compass'' for drawing circles that are larger than can be marked with a regular compass. Actually, you don't have to predrill the holes for the nail; just supply them as they are needed to suit the radius of the circle you need to draw. Figure 11-17 suggests an alternate method that is suitable for a particular radius. Use small clamps to secure a nail and a pencil to a strip of wood.

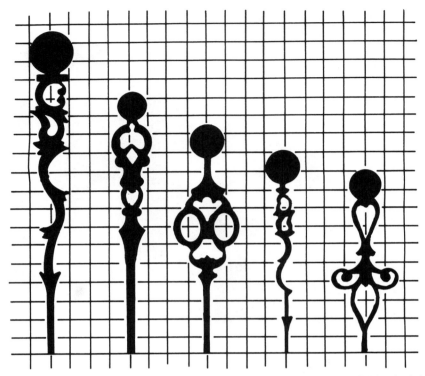

*Fig. 11-8.* These designs were produced on a copier by using readily available clock hands.

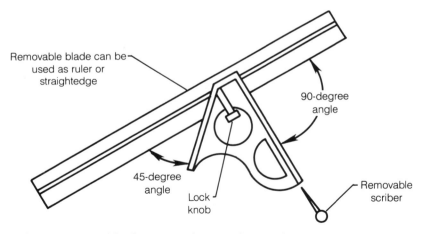

Removable blade can be
used as ruler or
straightedge

90-degree
angle

45-degree
angle

Lock
knob

Removable
scriber

*Fig. 11-9.* A common combination square lets you draw straight lines, check corner square-
ness, or mark 45-degree angles.

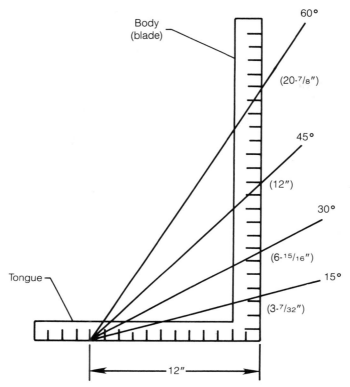

Fig. 11-10. A carpenter's square can be used to establish angles.

| No. Sides | Tongue dim. | Blade dim. |
|-----------|-------------|------------|
| 3         |             | $20\text{-}7/8''$ |
| 4         |             | 12 |
| 5         |             | $8\text{-}25/32$ |
| 6         |             | $6\text{-}15/16$ |
| 7         |             | $5\text{-}25/32$ |
| 8         |             | $3\text{-}31/32$ |
| 9         | $12''$      | $4\text{-}3/8$ |
| 10        |             | $3\text{-}7/8$ |
| 11        |             | $3\text{-}17/32$ |
| 12        |             | $3\text{-}7/32$ |
| 14        |             | $2\text{-}3/4$ |
| 16        |             | $2\text{-}13/32$ |
| 18        |             | $2\text{-}1/8$ |
| 20        |             | $1\text{-}29/32$ |

Example of a segmented assembly.

Fig. 11-11. Use the carpenter's square idea to determine the angle for segmented assemblies. The tongue is placed at the 12-inch mark on one edge of the stock. The adjacent edge is marked at the dimension that relates to the number of sides. A line that is drawn from the tongue to the blade tells the angle that is needed.

*Fig. 11-12.* A pair of dividers or a compass can be used to mark duplicate contours. Keep the point and pencil on a line that is perpendicular to the contour.

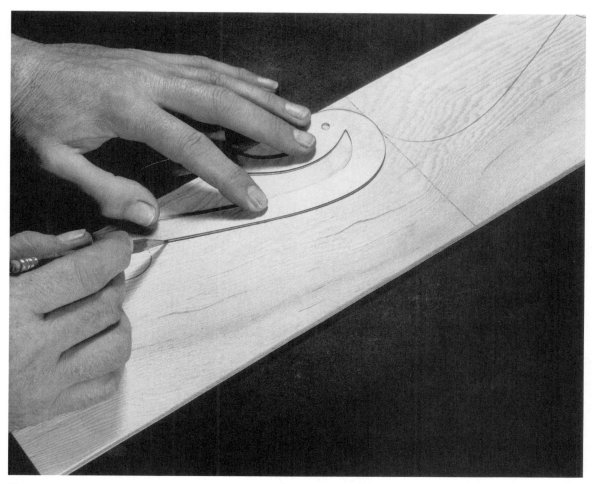

*Fig. 11-13.* A draftsman's French curve is a very practical layout tool.

## GEOMETRICAL CONSTRUCTIONS

Geometrical constructions offer a way to do precise layout work by using nothing more than a straightedge, a pencil, and a compass. The constructions can be done directly on the workpiece or on heavy paper that can then be used as a pattern or to transfer the results. Figures 11-18 through 11-27 offer many practical applications.

*Fig. 11-14.* All of these lines and patterns were drawn by tracing around various edges of a single French curve.

*Fig. 11-15.* Circle templates are available in various sizes. They make it easy to draw circles or to construct rounded corners.

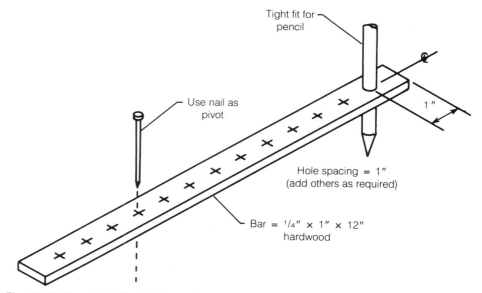

Tight fit for pencil

Use nail as pivot

Hole spacing = 1″
(add others as required)

1″

Bar = ¼″ × 1″ × 12″
hardwood

*Fig. 11-16.* A project like this is used to draw circles or arcs that are too large for a regular compass.

*Fig. 11-17.* You can improvise a ''compass'' by using small clamps to secure a nail and a pencil.

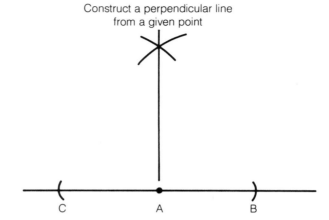

Construct a perpendicular line
from a given point

*Fig. 11-18.* How to construct a
perpendicular line from a given
point.

From base of perpendicular "A"
mark arcs "B" and "C"—open
compass and mark intersecting
arcs—line from "A" through
arcs will be perpendicular

Round off corners

Method One

Method Two

Set compass to radius of
arc and mark from "C" to
"A" and "B"—use "A" and "B"
as centers to draw intersecting
arcs that provide the center
for the round corner

Mark a square with sides
equal to the radius of the
curve—use inside corner
"A" as the center for the
round corner

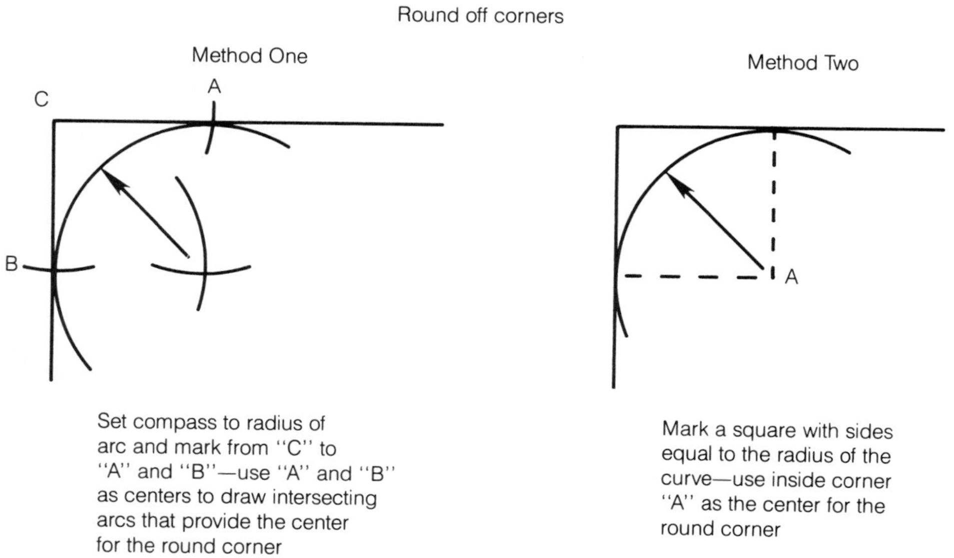

*Fig. 11-19.* The geometrical way to mark corners so they can be sawed to a uniform arc.

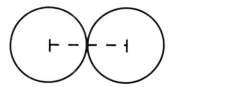 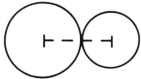

For abutting circles or arcs of similar size, the distance between centers = diameters—if circles differ, distance between centers is the sum of the radii

*Fig. 11-20.* How to do the layout for abutting circles whether or not they have similar diameters.

 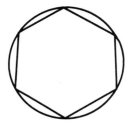 

5-Point star or
pentagon (72 degrees)

Hexagon
(60 degrees)

Octagon
(45 degrees)

*Fig. 11-21.* Constructions that are possible by using a circle as a starting point.

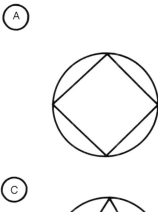

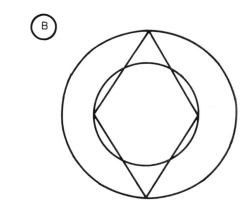

A—For perfect square, connect perpendicular diameters

B—Work with concentric circles for diamond shape

C—Form an equilateral triangle by connecting points 120 degrees apart

*Fig. 11-22.* The sizes of the patterns that you develop will depend on the diameter of the circle.

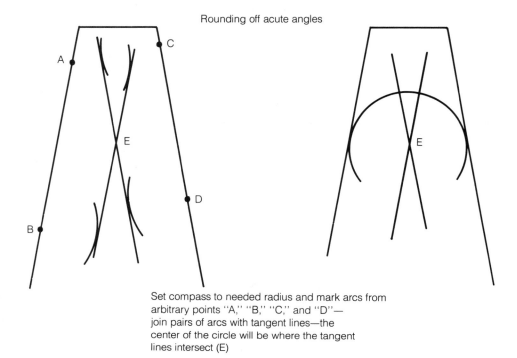

Rounding off acute angles

Set compass to needed radius and mark arcs from
arbitrary points "A," "B," "C," and "D"—
join pairs of arcs with tangent lines—the
center of the circle will be where the tangent
lines intersect (E)

*Fig. 11-23.* How to round off acute angles.

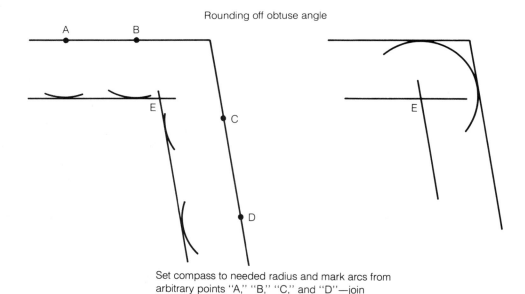

Rounding off obtuse angle

Set compass to needed radius and mark arcs from
arbitrary points "A," "B," "C," and "D"—join
pairs of arcs with tangent lines—the intersection
of the lines (E) will be the center of the circle

*Fig. 11-24.* How to round off obtuse angles.

238

S-curve

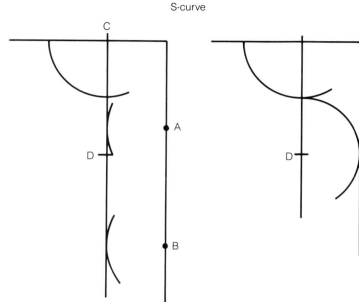

Fig. 11-25. You can draw a uniform S-curve by following these directions.

Set compass to needed radius and mark arcs from arbitrary points "A" and "B"—join arcs with tangent line and mark first arc from "C"—double compass setting and mark "D" from "C"—reset compass to original dimension and mark second arc using "D" as center

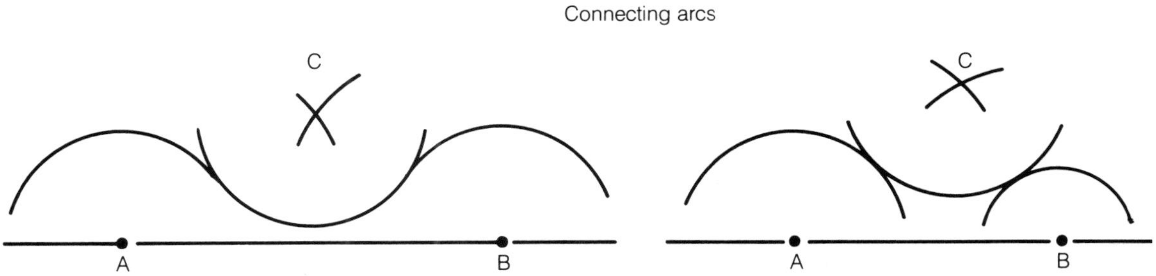

Connecting arcs

Set compass to radius of each arc plus radius of connecting arc and mark intersecting arcs "C" from points "A" and "B"—reset compass to needed arc and use "C" as center

Fig. 11-26. How to connect arcs.

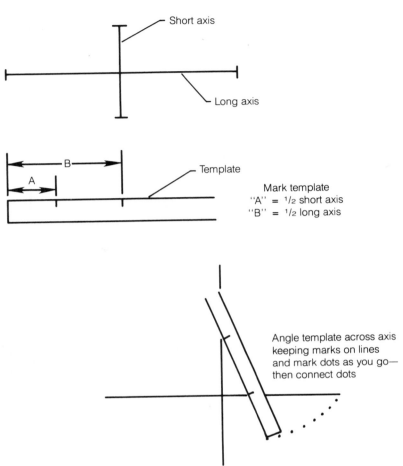

*Fig. 11-27.* How to draw an ellipse. The template is a length of wood or stiff cardboard.

# Chapter 12

# Project Section

**S**O YOU KNOW HOW TO USE A SCROLL SAW. NOW WHAT? THERE IS MUCH ENJOYMENT IN learning what the tool is and becoming acquainted with techniques that allow full use of the tool, but the real fun comes with using the knowledge to make projects. This chapter offers a good quantity and an ample variety of ideas that you can work on. Some are for practical purposes, such as a key rack or a breadboard. Others are toys, home decorations, gifts, or products to sell.

Except for some accessory operations that some projects might need, such as drilling a hole or forming a groove in a base, all of the ideas are scroll saw ventures. Of course, if there are other tools in the shop and you choose to involve them in some way, why not? You might want to smooth edges by using a drum sander in a drill press or by chucking it in a portable electric drill, that sort of thing.

There are options concerning the size of a project. Some of those that follow are marked with squares so you can duplicate or enlarge them by using the squares method that was explained in chapter 11. When the pattern isn't squared off, use the tracing paper method to copy it and then enlarge it on a second sheet that will serve as a pattern. Don't overlook the suggestion about using a copying machine. You can make copies directly from the book and then enlarge them.

Finishing is optional. You can use paint or stain or leave the material natural. Choose a material you feel will suit the project—plywood, hardboard, hardwood; there are many choices. Toy cars and cutting boards deserve a hardwood, such as maple or birch that are best left natural. Certainly, don't use a toxic material on anything a child will play with. Bread boards or cutting boards can be coated with a special salad bowl finish or with several applications of mineral oil. Don't use a cooking oil because it can turn rancid.

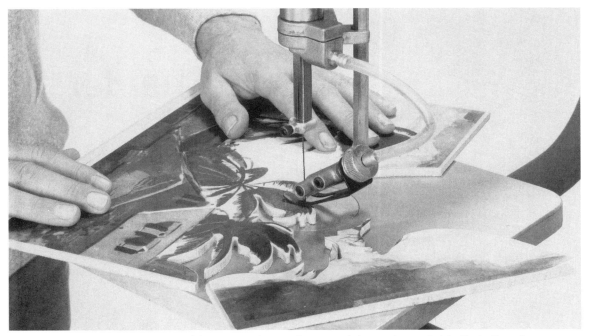

*Fig. 12-1.* The quickest way to provide patterns for scroll-saw work is to adopt suitable illustrations from magazines and other periodicals. They can be produced in profile shape or sawed as jigsaw puzzles.

Some projects can be embellished by applying paint or by woodburning to show details. It's sometimes best to paint in facial features. Using round or oval holes for eyes isn't always the best way to go.

In addition to what you will find in this book, there are countless sources of ready-to-use patterns. Illustrations can be taken from magazines and other periodicals and attached to the project material with spray adhesive or rubber cement (Fig. 12-1). Don't overlook nature as a library of patterns. The designs in Fig. 12-2 were traced directly from leaves taken from various trees.

## USING A PROJECT

There are various ways to display projects. We'll use the horse pattern shown in Fig. 12-3 as an example. It can be used as is after scroll sawing, attaching it to a wall with, say, double-face tape, or it can stand independently by providing it with a base (Fig. 12-4). The base, which can be any shape, can be grooved to accept the project or you can use twin strips of wood to serve the same purpose (Fig. 12-5). Projects can be overlaid on a backing to give them more emphasis. The backing can be formal or not as demonstrated in Figs. 12-6 and 12-7. In Fig. 12-7, the horse served as a template so a portable router could be used to outline it and so provide additional design detail.

*Fig. 12-2.* Nature's bounty includes patterns for the scroll saw.

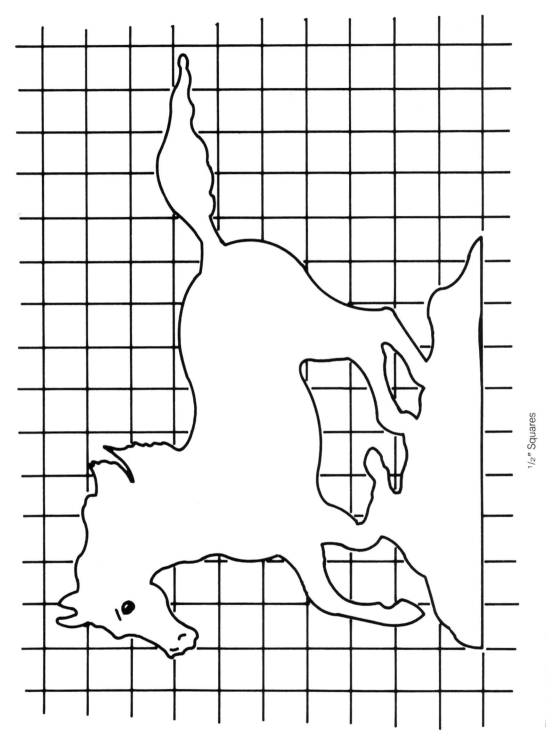

$^1/_2$" Squares

*Fig. 12-3.* Horse plaque.

*Fig. 12-4.* Many projects can be used like statuettes if you supply a base to hold them vertically.

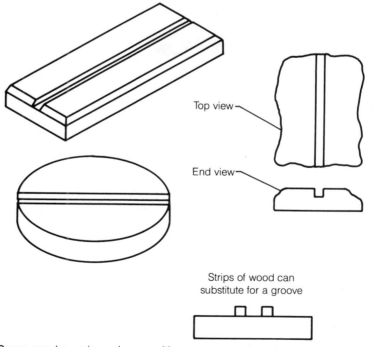

Top view—

End view—

Strips of wood can
substitute for a groove

*Fig. 12-5.* Bases can be various shapes with grooves or strips of wood to secure the project.

*Fig. 12-6.* Projects can be mounted on a backing so they appear framed like a picture. Attach the project with glue; nails are not needed. A chamfered edge adds to the project's appearance.

*Fig. 12-7.* The shape of a mounting piece is optional. A portable router with a small round-end bit was used to trace around the project. The extra touch adds depth.

## A 3-D IDEA

Some projects, especially animal figures, take on an extra dimension when parts of the body are cut separately and then added to the main part (Fig. 12-8). Assembling is done with drops of woodworking glue and brads. Set the brads below the surface of the wood and fill the holes with a wood dough. The plan for the pig project is offered in Fig. 12-9. Notice that the tail can be a solid piece.

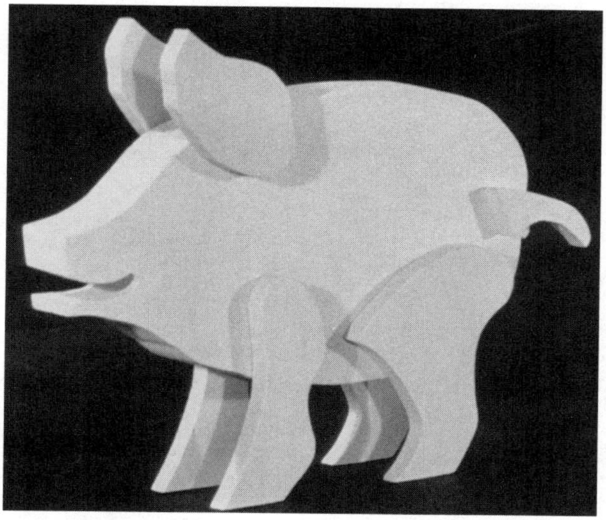

*Fig. 12-8.* 3-D projects are created by sawing some body parts separately and then adding them to the main part.

## KERFED DETAILS

It's often better to provide particular details on projects by using a fine kerf rather than supplying a line by painting or woodburning. The boat project in Fig. 12-10 offers a chance to demonstrate the idea. The boat could be displayed as is, but doing a fine-line piercing job shows the water line across the hull (Fig. 12-11). The project then says, one hundred percent scroll saw work.

## A LARGE PROJECT

The idea shown in Fig. 12-12 is included to make the point that scroll saw projects don't all have to be small. The project will stand 39 inches tall and will make a nice decoration for a child's room. Add some practicality by inserting a few dowels in the brow area. Then it can serve as a clothes hanger. This is typical of projects that can be enhanced by doing a colorful paint job, but be sure to use a nontoxic finishing material.

## SOME PRACTICAL PROJECTS

Use 1 1/2-inch-thick maple or birch for the cutting board (Fig. 12-13). If you have trouble finding a hardwood that is 12 inches wide, select a couple or narrower pieces and glue them edge to edge to form the base stock.

Legs and ears cut separately
and attached to body

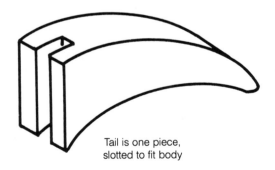

Tail is one piece,
slotted to fit body

*Fig. 12-9.* Pattern for the 3-D pig project. Note that the tail can be one piece.

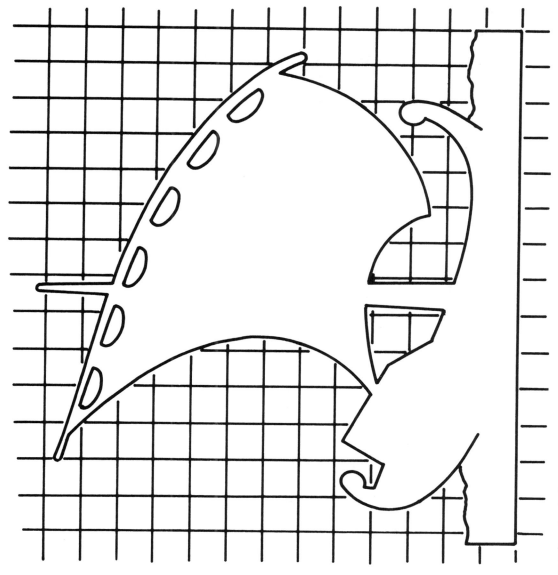

*Fig. 12-10.* Pattern for a boat plaque.

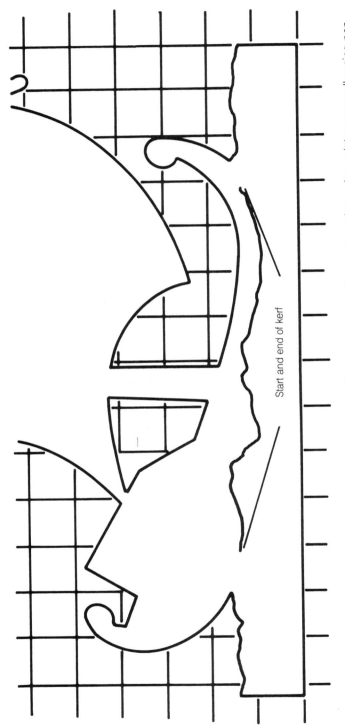

Start and end of kerf

*Fig. 12-11.* Details can be added to many projects by using a pierced kerf. It's often a better way to go than using paint or a woodburning pen.

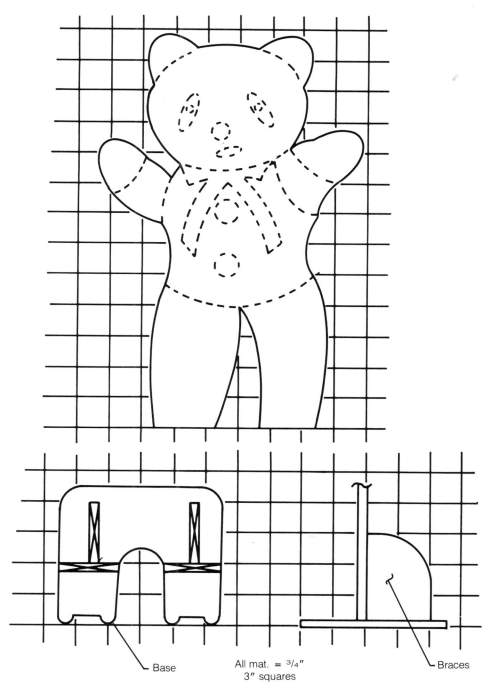

Base

All mat. = ³/₄″
3″ squares

Braces

*Fig. 12-12.* This bear project will stand about 39 inches tall. Use glue and flathead wood screws to assemble components. Dotted lines indicate features that can be painted.

Cutting board

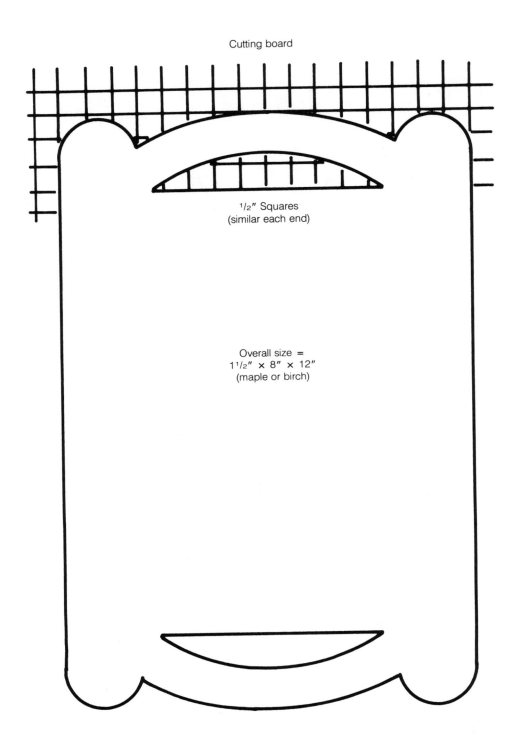

1/2" Squares
(similar each end)

Overall size =
1 1/2" × 8" × 12"
(maple or birch)

*Fig. 12-13.* Pattern for a cutting board.

The breadboard (Fig. 12-14) also should be made of hardwood, but stock that is 3/4-inch thick will do.

A soft wood, such as pine, can be used for the key rack and the welcome sign (Figs. 12-15 and 12-16).

## TOY CARS

Wooden toy cars are very popular items, not only for children, but as sale products to local stores, at fairs, and flea markets. That's why we offer quite a few patterns (Figs. 12-17 through 12-21). It's best to use a wood that will take some abuse, like 3/4-inch or 1 1/2-inch maple or birch. Do a good sanding job and use sandpaper wrapped around a block of wood to round off corners. A natural finish is appropriate for the projects.

The cars need wheels (Fig. 12-22), and they can be sawed out on the scroll saw, but when you need many of them it's best to work in other ways. Hole saws speed production if a drill press is available, or you can take advantage of ready-made wheels that are offered in many craftsman's catalogs. They come in various sizes and some are shaped to appear more realistic.

## PUZZLES

The popular jigsaw puzzle is, of course, a natural for scroll saw work. Best bet here is to find suitable illustrations or photos and attach them to a backing of thin cabinet grade plywood, hardboard, or stiff posterboard. Sawing can be done randomly or by producing interlocking pieces (Fig. 12-23).

Other puzzles that are really designed for children can be made as shown in Fig. 12-24. Once the pattern is sawed to outline shape, you do more sawing to create individual pieces. Work with 1/4-inch or 1/2-inch hardwood.

## PATTERNS FOR HOLIDAYS

Patterns for holidays are especially good for cottage industry products. Figures that are used can be realistic or whimsical. Because comparatively thin material can be used (1/8 inch to 1/4 inch), don't overlook the pad-sawing method for producing in quantity.

For Halloween ideas see Figs. 12-25 and 12-26.
Easter ideas are offered in Figs. 12-27 through 12-29.
For Christmas check Fig. 12-30.
Valentine hearts are detailed in Fig. 12-31.

## SHELF BRACKETS

To make shelf brackets, select material and its thickness to accommodate what the shelf must support. The designs shown in Figs. 12-32 and 12-33 require some piercing; those in Fig. 12-34 can be cut faster because they involve only profile sawing.

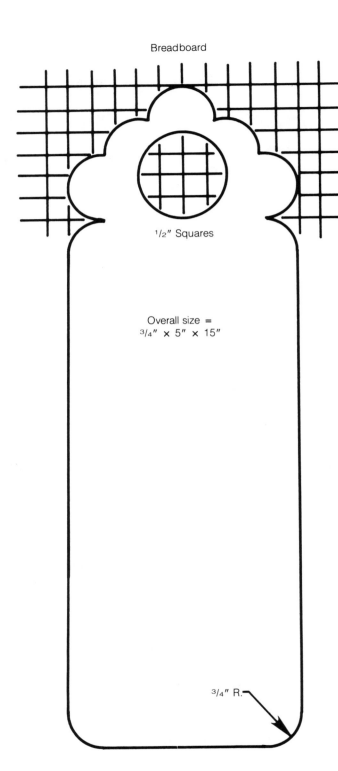

Breadboard

1/2″ Squares

Overall size =
3/4″ × 5″ × 15″

*Fig. 12-14.* Pattern for a bread board.

3/4″ R.

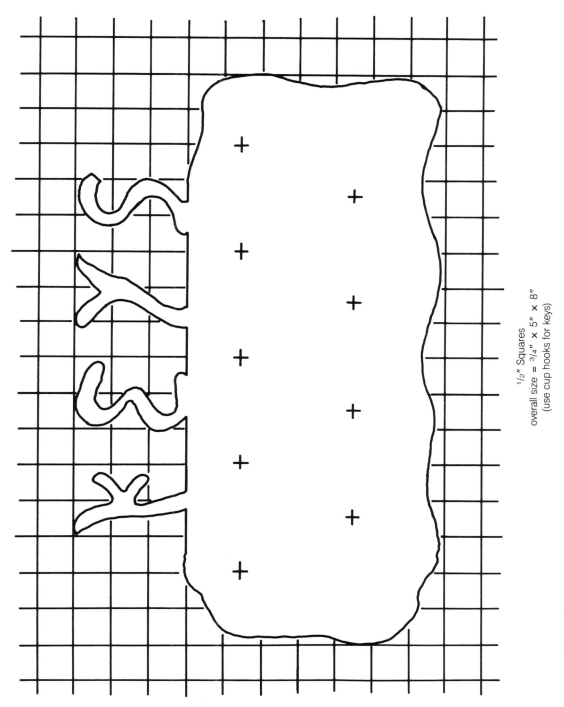

'1/2" Squares
overall size = 3/4" × 5" × 8"
(use cup hooks for keys)

*Fig. 12-15.* Clear pine is a good material for projects like this key rack. Apply a clear finish or paint it to suit existing decor.

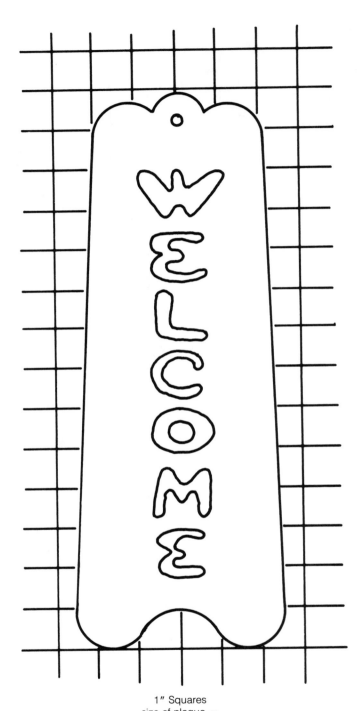

*Fig. 12-16.* The welcome sign should have several applications of an exterior-type sealer if it is used outdoors. All letters are done by piercing.

1″ Squares
size of plaque =
³/₄″ × 5″ × 14″

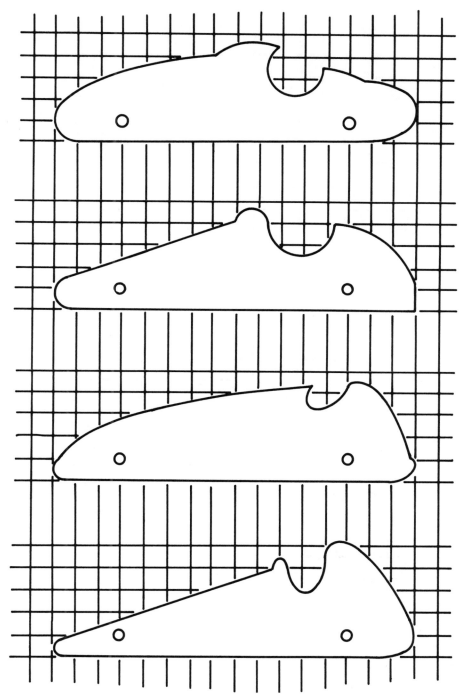

*Fig. 12-17.* Car selection #1. Many patterns are offered because this type of project is a prime cottage industry product.

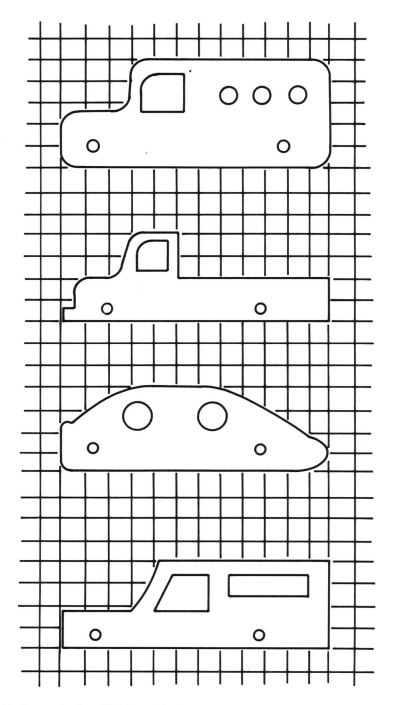

*Fig. 12-18.* Care selection #2. Using 1-inch squares when transferring the patterns will produce cars about 12 inches long.

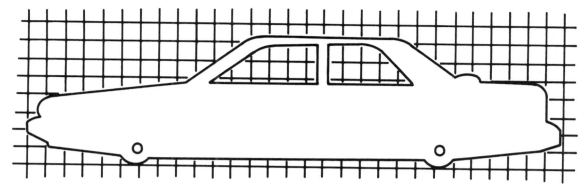

*Fig. 12-19.* Car profiles can be more detailed. This project will be about 15 inches long if you use ¹/₂-inch squares.

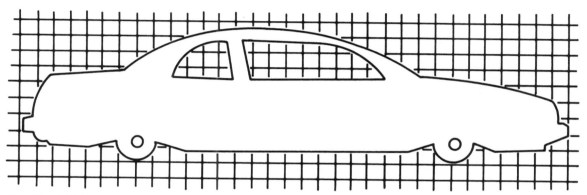

*Fig. 12-20.* This car project will be about 9 inches long if you use ¹/₄-inch squares.

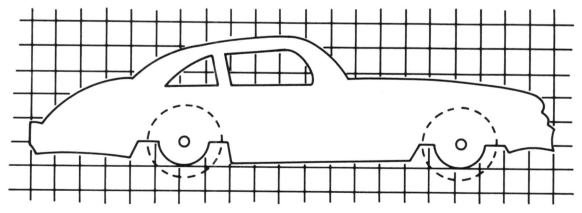

*Fig. 12-21.* Use ¹/₂-inch squares for this car project to be about 11 inches long. Windows on car projects can be outlined with a woodburning pen or painted if you wish to avoid a piercing procedure.

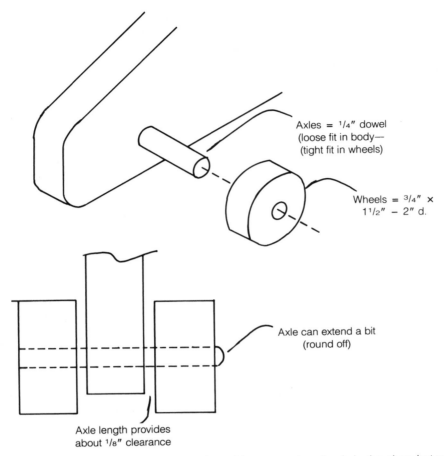

Axles = ¼" dowel
(loose fit in body—
(tight fit in wheels)

Wheels = ¾" ×
1½" – 2" d.

Axle can extend a bit
(round off)

Axle length provides
about ⅛" clearance

*Fig. 12-22.* How to add wheels to car projects. You can make wheels in the shop but when they are needed in quantity it's better to buy them readymade.

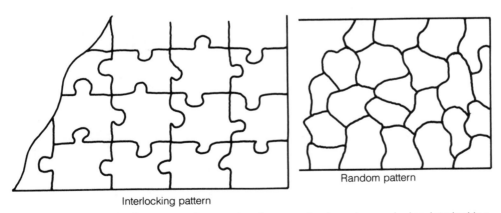

Interlocking pattern

Random pattern

*Fig. 12-23.* Sawing for jigsaw puzzles can be done randomly or by producing interlocking pieces.

1″ Squares

Sawed on dotted lines after
profile is shaped

*Fig. 12-24.* Puzzles for children
are produced by sawing a
completed project into a number of individual parts. Dotted
lines suggest a sawing pattern.

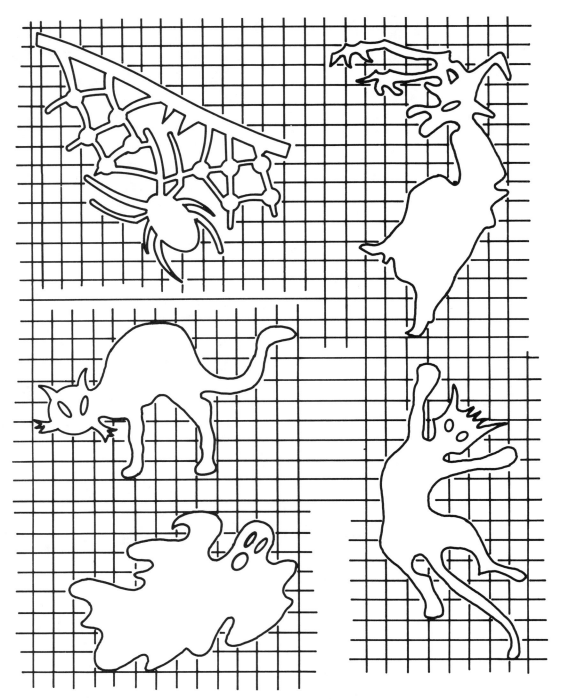

**Fig. 12-25.** Patterns for Halloween. The projects can be large or small. If small, you can epoxy a jewelry finding to the back so they can be worn like pins. You can embellish with felt pens or poster paints.

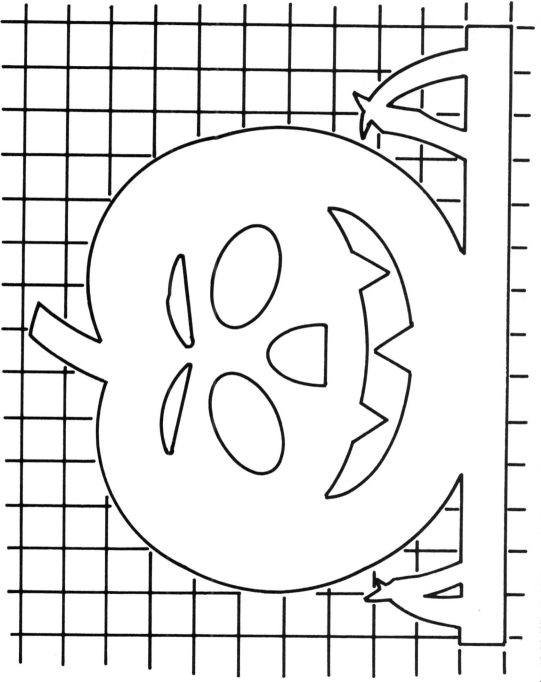

*Fig. 12-26.* What is Halloween (or Thanksgiving) without a pumpkin? Make two; place one on the lawn and hang one in a window. Use ³/₄-inch exterior grade plywood. Paint bright orange. Do piercing or use a black felt-tip marking pen for features.

*Fig. 12-27.* Bunnies are for Easter.

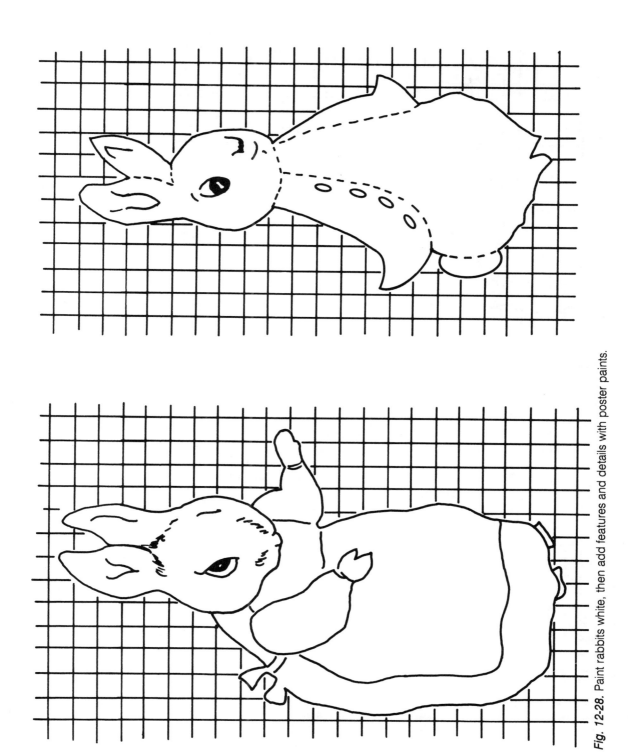

*Fig. 12-28.* Paint rabbits white, then add features and details with poster paints.

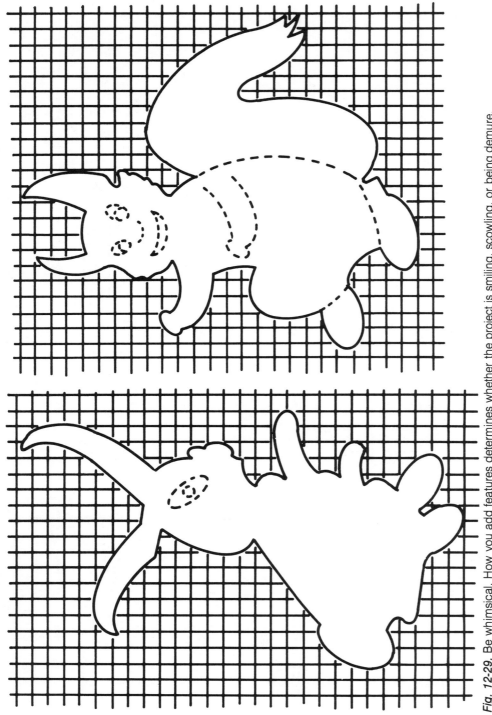

*Fig. 12-29.* Be whimsical. How you add features determines whether the project is smiling, scowling, or being demure.

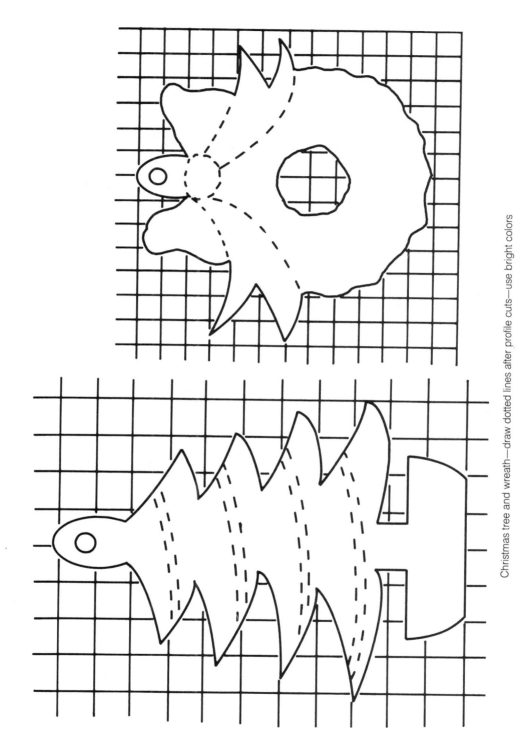

Christmas tree and wreath—draw dotted lines after profile cuts—use bright colors

*Fig. 12-30.* Projects for Christmas. If you choose to make these in very large sizes, you can saw them as half pieces and then glue the parts together.

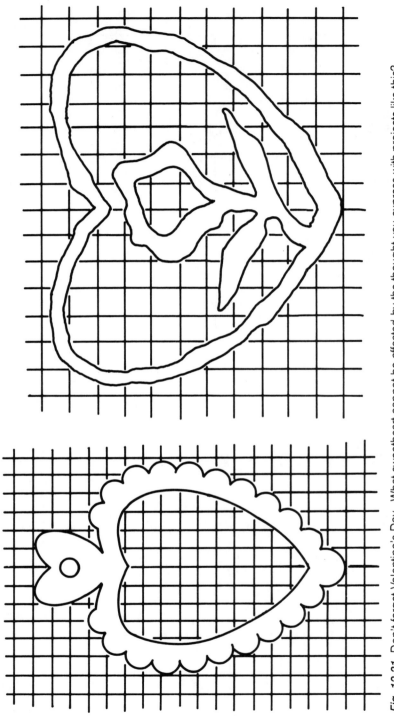

Fig. 12-31. Don't forget Valentine's Day. What sweetheart cannot be affected by the thought you express with projects like this?

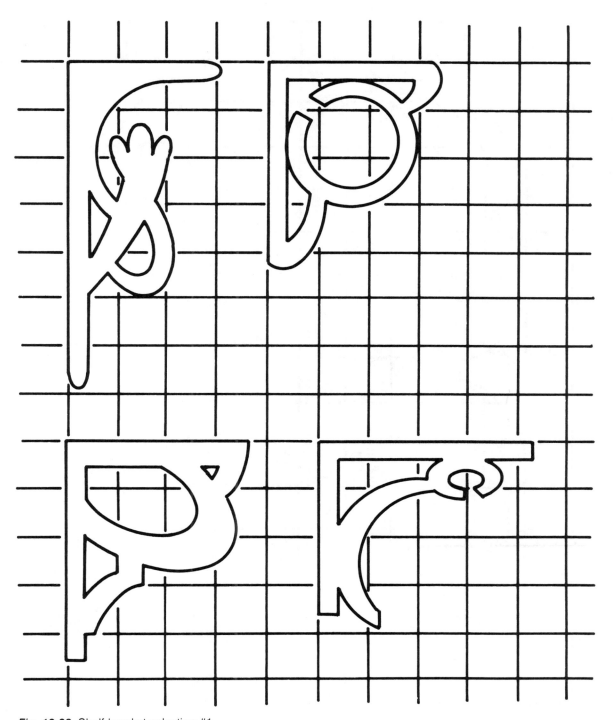

*Fig. 12-32.* Shelf bracket selection #1.

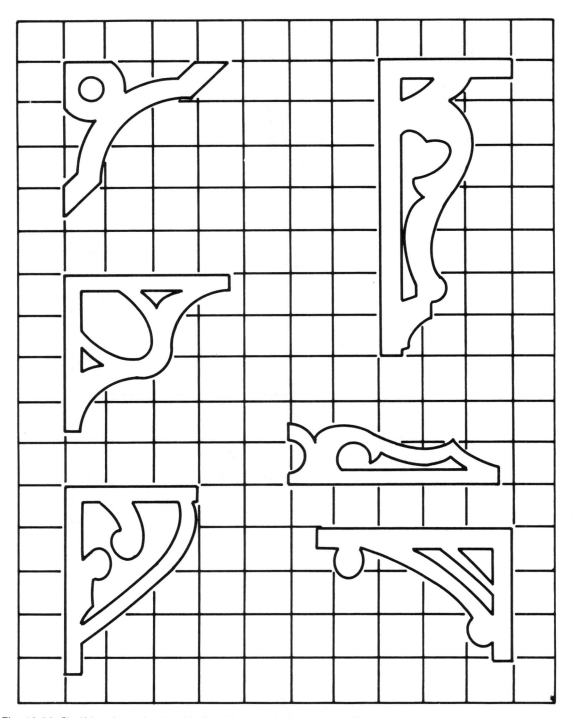

*Fig. 12-33.* Shelf bracket selection #2. As with those in the previous illustration, these projects require piercing.

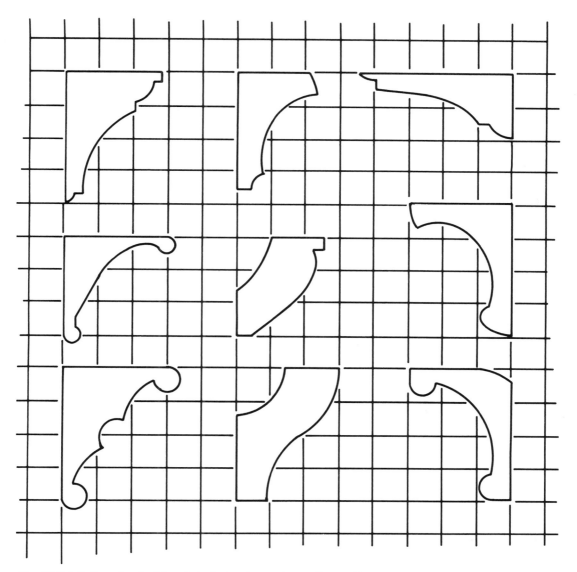

*Fig. 12-34.* Pattern for shelf brackets that only require profile sawing.

## WILDLIFE PATTERNS

Figures of wildlife, birds and beasts and such, can be realistic or whimsical, even surrealistic. It's fun to experiment, to duplicate as closely as possible a real life presence, or to represent by being guided by your imagination. Figures 12-35 through 12-43 offer an ample supply of patterns to consider. Note that some are straight profiles while others have integral frames. You can choose to go one way or the other. Skip the frame if one is shown, or add it when one is lacking.

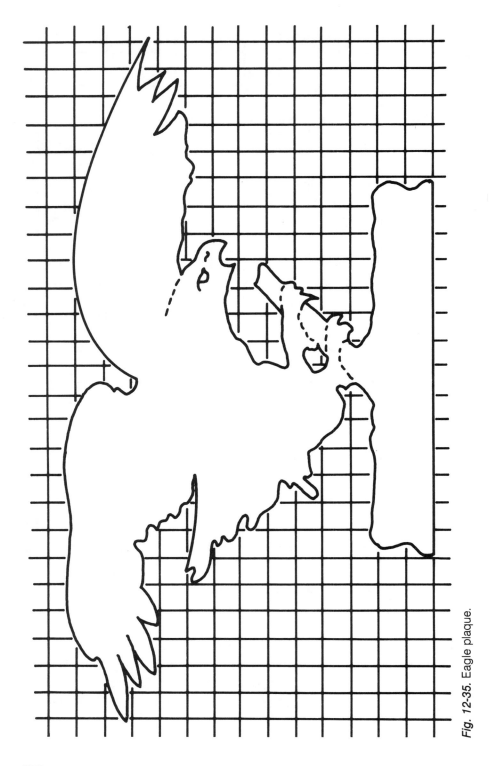

*Fig. 12-35.* Eagle plaque.

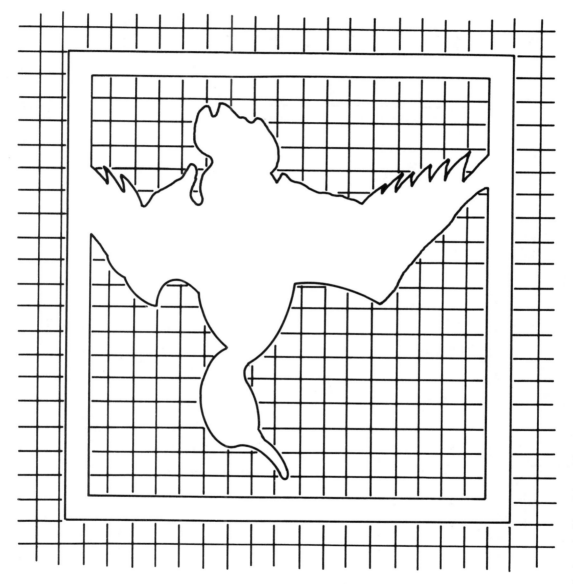

*Fig. 12-36.* Duck project has integral frame.

*Fig. 12-37.* Framed swan and moon is also a one-piece project.

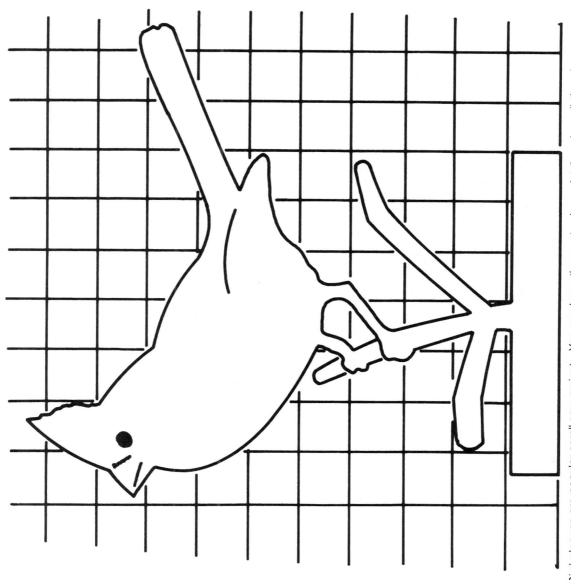

*Fig. 12-38.* Bird plaques are popular scroll-saw projects. You can leave them natural or paint them in realistic colors.

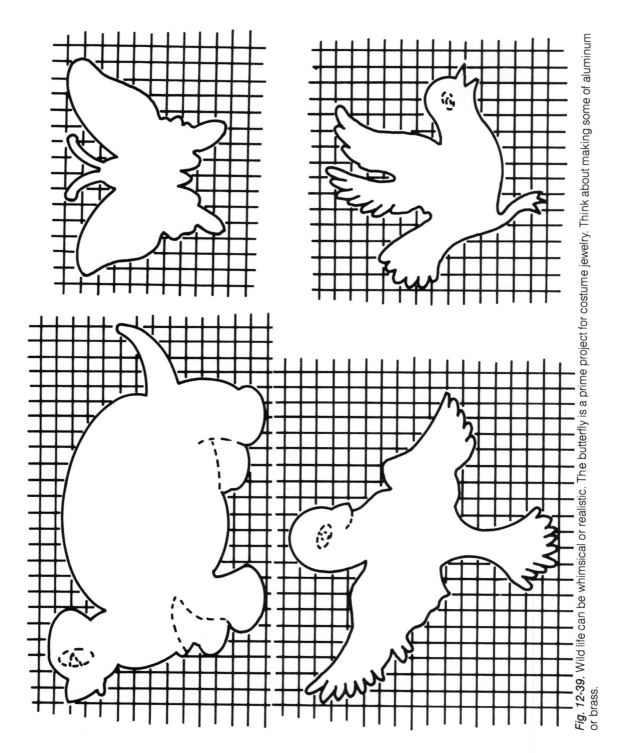

Fig. 12-39. Wild life can be whimsical or realistic. The butterfly is a prime project for costume jewelry. Think about making some of aluminum or brass.

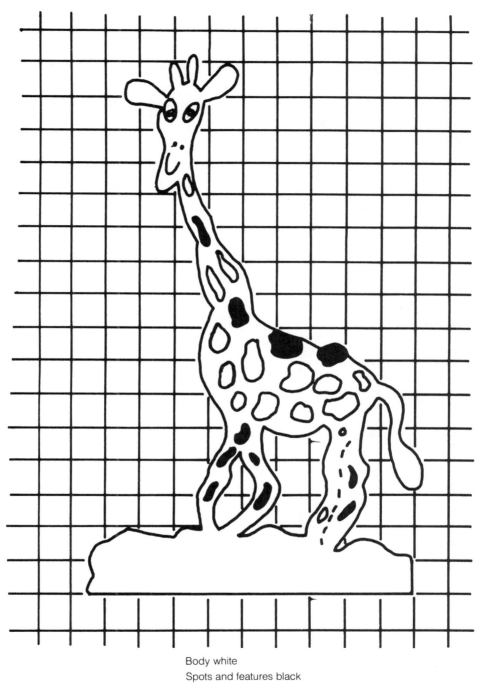

Body white
Spots and features black

*Fig. 12-40.* The giraffe is another project to think of in large size as a decoration for a child's room.

*Fig. 12-41.* A horse right out of mythology.

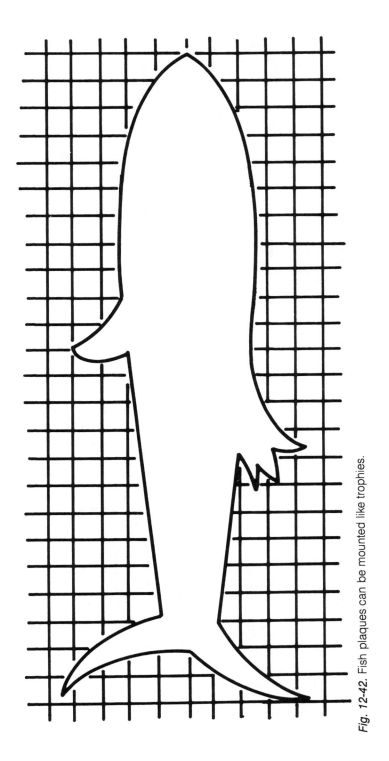

*Fig. 12-42.* Fish plaques can be mounted like trophies.

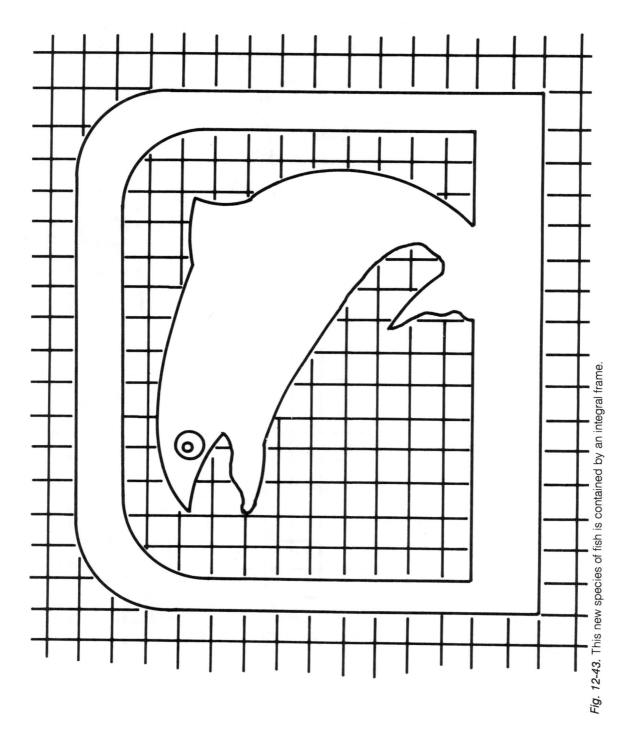

*Fig. 12-43.* This new species of fish is contained by an integral frame.

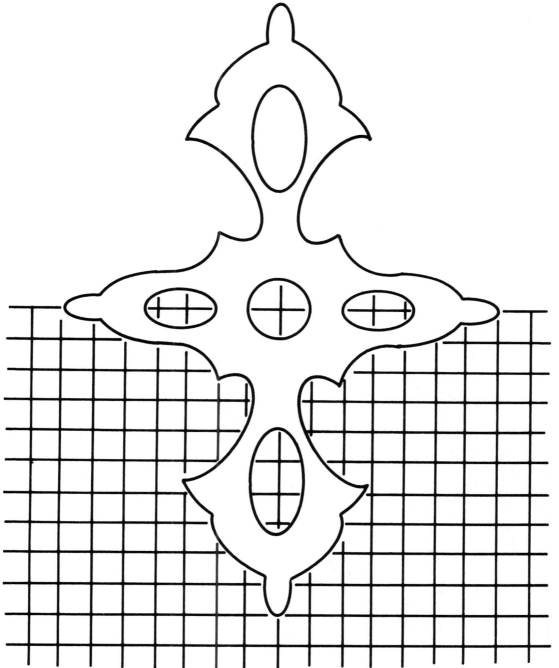

*Fig. 12-44.* Escutcheons can be used as overlays or inlays. Inlaying requires very careful recessing in the parent project.

## ESCUTCHEON DESIGNS

There are different interpretations of "escutcheons," but for our purposes they are scroll-sawed patterns that can be inlaid or overlaid to enhance a project. They can be used, for example, as a design detail around a door lock or even a switch plate. Often, escutcheons are made of prosaic or precious metals and used to decorate jewelry boxes. Some ideas are offered in Figs. 12-44 through 12-46.

## MISCELLANEOUS PROJECTS

There are so many roads to travel when choosing a project for the scroll saw. Figures 12-47 through 12-55 offer some lanes and highways that you can travel on.

## NUMBERS AND LETTERS

There are so many ways to go when designing numbers and letters. Sketch them out in almost haphazard fashion, see them as italics, or, as illustrated in Figs. 12-56 and 12-57, be rather formal. What you produce can be mounted on plain board, or you can go a bit further by making a special mounting plaque like the one shown in Fig. 12-58. A thought, when doing projects like this, is that when you need duplicates you can produce them with a single sawing procedure on thick stock and then resaw to get more than one (Fig. 12-59). If the size of the figure permits, you can do the work on the scroll saw by using a heavy blade. A band saw, if one is available, will do a good job on oversize pieces. Also, if neither of these suggestions will work, you can slice apart the original project by using a handsaw.

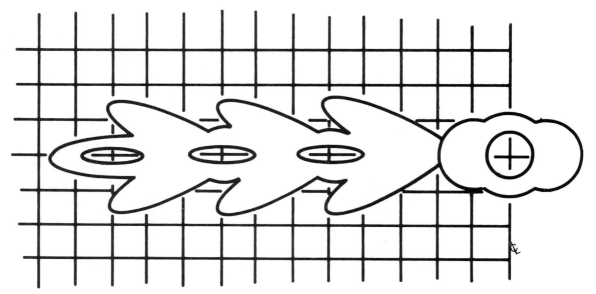

*Fig. 12-45.* Escutcheons can be made of wood or metal.

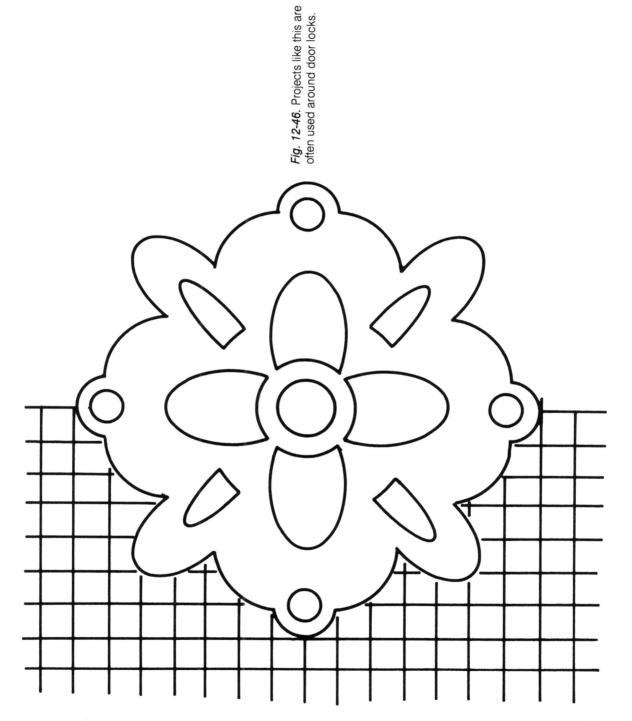

*Fig. 12-46.* Projects like this are often used around door locks.

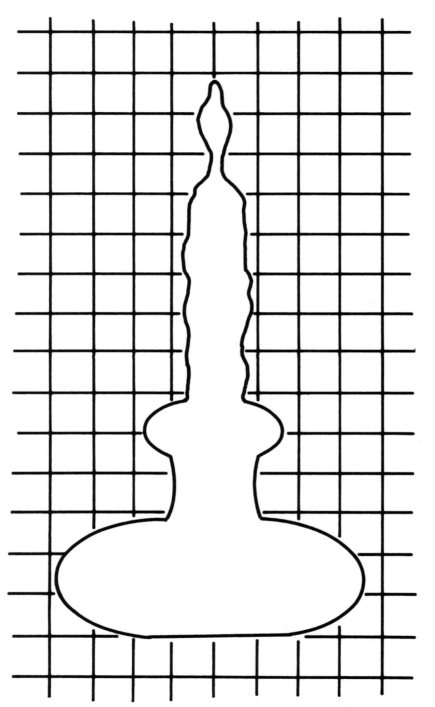

*Fig. 12-47.* Consider this candlestick as a project for inlaying. It was shown in chapter 8.

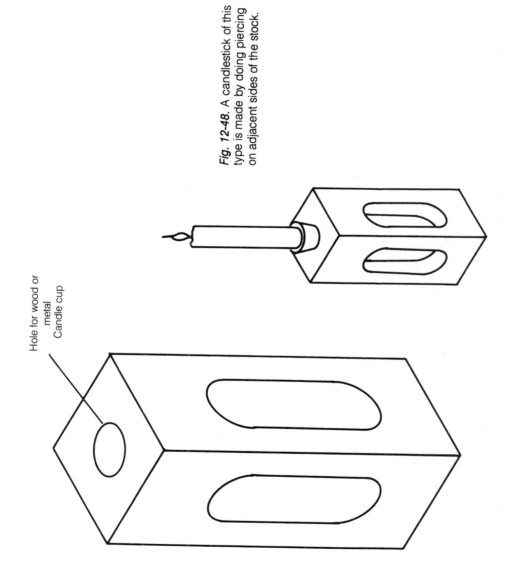

Hole for wood or
metal
Candle cup

Fig. 12-48. A candlestick of this type is made by doing piercing on adjacent sides of the stock.

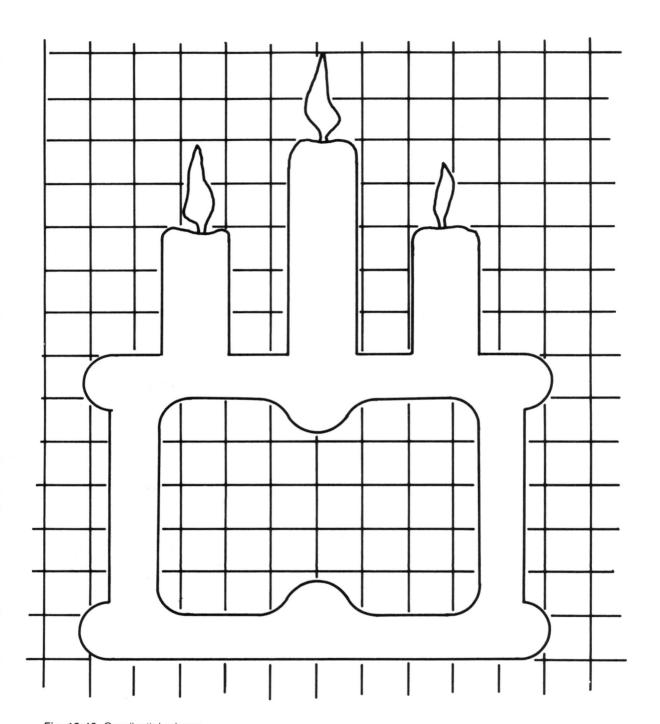

*Fig. 12-49.* Candlestick plaque.

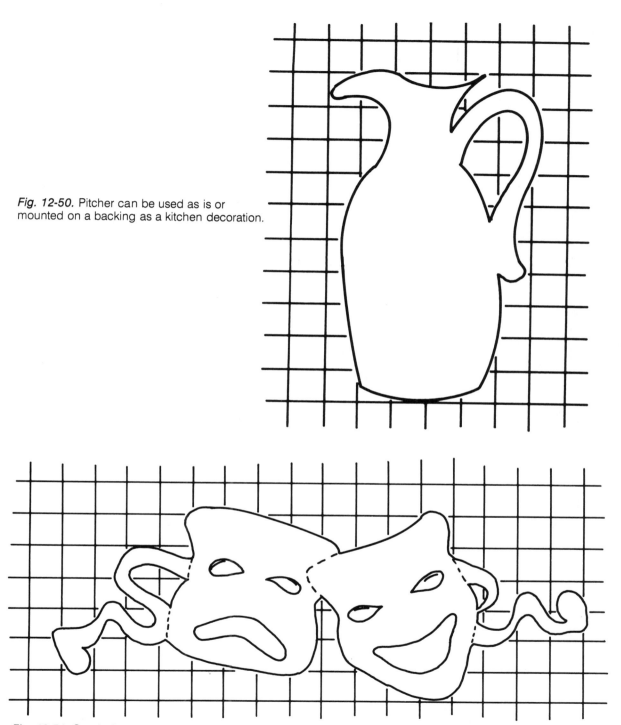

*Fig. 12-50.* Pitcher can be used as is or mounted on a backing as a kitchen decoration.

*Fig. 12-51.* Carnival masque.

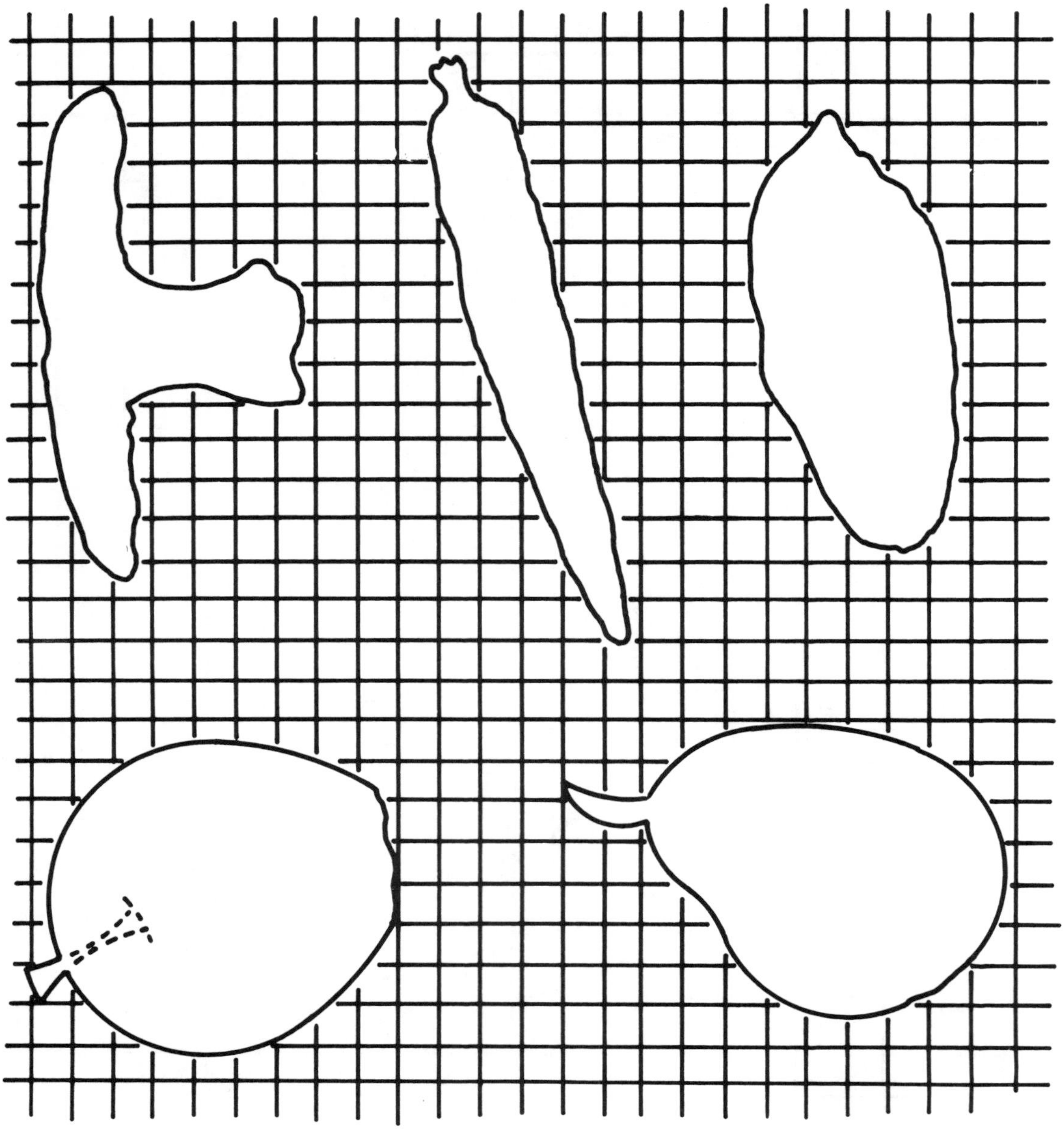

*Fig. 12-52.* Fruit and vegetables.

*Fig. 12-53.* Framed flowers.

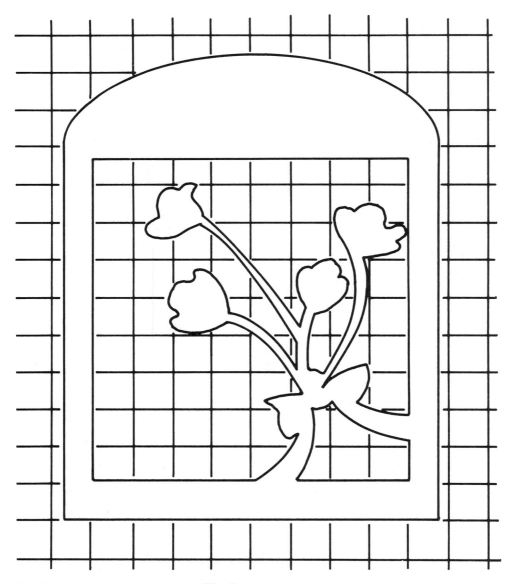

*Fig. 12-54.* Designs of frames can differ. Does this look like flowers in a window?

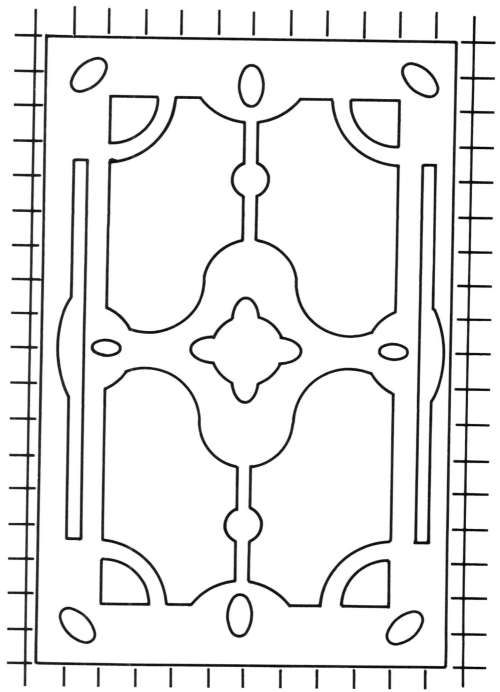

*Fig. 12-55.* This project has many uses. Think of hinging a few as a small, table-top screen. How about a door on a small project? Use it vertically or horizontally.

ABCDEF
GHIJKLM
NOPQRS
TUVWXY
Z 12345
67890

*Fig. 12-56.* Alphabet #1. Letters and numbers are on the formal side and meant to be sawed individually for mounting on a board.

A B C D E F G H I
J K L M N O P Q
R S T U V W X Y
Z $ 1 2 3 4 5
¢ 6 7 8 9 0

*Fig. 12-57.* Alphabet # 2.

292

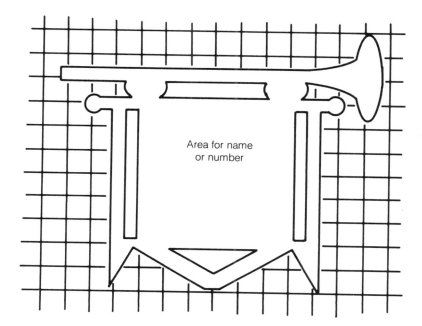

Area for name
or number

*Fig. 12-58.* You can be fancy with how you arrange to mount house numbers or names.

*Fig. 12-59.* Resawing will create duplicates when you need more than one letter or number. You can work with a heavy blade on a scroll saw if work size allows. Call on the band saw if one is available. As a last resort, use a handsaw to do the separating.

# Index